Strings Attached

Strings Attached

Untangling the Ethics of Incentives

Ruth W. Grant

RUSSELL SAGE FOUNDATION • NEW YORK

PRINCETON UNIVERSITY PRESS • PRINCETON AND OXFORD

Library of Congress Cataloging-in-Publication Data

Grant, Ruth Weissbourd, 1951–
Strings attached : untangling the ethics of incentives / Ruth W. Grant.
p. cm.
Includes bibliographical references and index.
ISBN 978-0-691-15160-1 (hardcover : alk. paper)
1. Incentive (Psychology) 2. Motivation (Psychology) 3. Political psychology.
4. Political ethics. I. Title.
JA74.5.G73 2011
170—dc22
2011011921

British Library Cataloging-in-Publication Data is available
This book has been composed in Sabon Lt std
Printed on acid-free paper.∞
Printed in the United States of America
1 3 5 7 9 10 8 6 4 2

To Steve

Contents

Preface

THE IDEA FOR THIS PROJECT was born during an undergraduate seminar in ancient Greek political philosophy. The students were exploring the circumstances under which coercion, or force, might be ethically superior to persuasion. That possibility ran counter to their usual assumptions. How often had they been told as youngsters to "use your words" instead of hitting or pushing or grabbing? The assigned reading for that day was the opening scene of Sophocles' *Philoctetes*. Philoctetes is in possession of Achilles' bow, which the Greeks must have in order to defeat the Trojans. Odysseus, always the clever one, is attempting to persuade the noble young son of Achilles, Neoptolemus, to help him retrieve the bow by means of a deceitful scheme. Neoptolemus resists the use of such shameful tactics, saying,

> I have a natural antipathy to get my ends by tricks and strategems . . . Philoctetes I will gladly fight and capture, bring him with us, but not by treachery.[1]

For Neoptolemus, force is more honorable than fraud as a means of attaining one's goals.

And then someone asked, "What about incentives? Wouldn't that be an alternative way of getting Philoctetes to relinquish the bow?" Here was an interesting possibility; and even more interesting, it was a possibility that was not included in the play. Why not? Did the Greeks not understand that "everyone has his price"? Or, on the contrary, did they understand the limits to that saying better than we do? It is unlikely that an incentive would have worked with Philoctetes. Bargaining is not always an effective mode of influence. Resentment, pride, and a sense of honor all would prevent a successful negotiation in this case. One would expect that Philoctetes would not yield at any price. Indeed, acting honorably might be understood precisely as holding fast to those things that must be defended at any cost. Bargaining, like coercion and persuasion, involves ethical considerations too, it seems.

For whatever reason, the play does not include offering incentives as one possible approach to the problem of retrieving Achilles' bow. Instead, the possibilities are presented in terms of the dichotomy between speech and deed, persuasion and force. To be sure, persuasion includes explaining to Philoctetes the relative advantages and disadvantages of the choice he faces later in the play. If he relinquishes the bow and goes to Troy, certain things will follow as a matter of course: for example, he will have access to medical care for his wounded foot. But this is the natural consequence of a certain decision, not an incentive added as an inducement to make that decision.

I walked out of class thinking about incentives in a different way than I had before. Incentives now appeared as one kind of power separate from coercion and persuasion, and I found myself wondering how to judge the ethics of employing one kind rather than another. When is the use of force legitimate? What sorts of persuasion are illegitimate? How can legitimate uses of incentives be distinguished from illegitimate ones—bribery or blackmail, for example?

It is this last question that became the central question of this book. And the framework for my investigation has remained unchanged since that first day. By this I mean that incentives are construed as an exercise of power throughout the book. They are one of the means employed to get people to do what they otherwise would not. And incentives, like all kinds of power, are subject to abuse. This understanding brings the ethical issues involved with the use of incentives to the fore much more effectively than the alternative approach, according to which incentives are understood in the same terms as any other form of trade.

Many ideas may occur to a writer, but few grab you enough to stick with them through the process of writing a book. When they do, it is generally because they engage not only ongoing intellectual interests but also ongoing personal ambivalences and intersecting concerns. One day, while working on this book, a childhood memory came back to me. I was shopping with my mother in Marshall Field's department store in Chicago. The saleslady was very attentive, and we took some clothes into the dressing room to try on. As we did so, the saleslady said, "Remember, my name is Betty." In my naïveté, I thought that all of this was very nice. My mother's reaction was not so positive, and she explained to me that the salesladies worked on commission, a situation that pitted them against their fellow workers and encouraged them to flatter us. Betty would only receive her commission on the sale if we remembered to seek her out so that she could be the one to ring up the sale at the cash register. I recognize now in my mother's remarks a distant echo of the labor union attitudes toward incentives that first developed when incentives were introduced in the early twentieth century as part of a move toward "scientific management" in American industry. That story is briefly sketched in chapter 2.

In my case, the intellectual issue of ethics and incentives, once it had surfaced in the *Philoctetes* class, reverberated with my own experience: with my own sense of manipulation in certain situations where incentives were deployed; with my observation of the tensions between individual incentives and the cooperative spirit within institutions; and with my longstanding concerns about the use of incentives in education and child rearing. I found, for example, that people became more reluctant to "pitch in" in the workplace for the common benefit once it became the usual practice to offer some kind of bonus for any "extra" duty. I wondered what kind of lesson my child was learning from the teacher who gave extra credit on spelling tests to children who did not ask to use the bathroom. On account of a variety of experiences like these, the issue had been on my mind in one form or another for quite awhile, and this project took hold.

As I worked on this book, the very large philosophical questions of the possibility of ethical reasoning and the grounds of ethical judgment increasingly nagged in my ear. The book is meant to persuade the reader that there are certain ethical standards by which the use of incentives ought to be judged. Where do those standards come from? Do they apply across cultures? What "counts" as a good argument in matters of ethical judgment? What does it mean to have good judgment and how does one acquire it? Is knowledge possible in this area, or must ethical judgments necessarily be made in the absence of certainty and without conclusive demonstration?

These questions receive no direct answers here. Although, in principle, they are prior to and foundational for the sort of argument I present, I did not begin by answering them. Instead, I began with my own "gut reactions" and then subjected them to examination. As I worked through this process, the grounds of my opinions became clearer and some of them were altered; my understanding of incentives was sharpened; and I changed my mind about the ethics of their application in many areas. I hope that the reader will have a similar experience. Having begun with a suspicious attitude concerning the use of incentives, I found myself actually more hospitable to their use than many people in certain sorts of cases, for example, in the use of incentives to attract research subjects for medical research. Here is one area where my intuitive response was more favorable than the prevailing attitudes in the medical community, and the challenge for me was to appreciate the force of their critique.

As enlightening as this journey has been, I am well aware that this sort of analysis does not ground ethical principles down to bedrock. I do not offer a complete philosophical defense of the ethical perspective I develop in this book. Some crucial premises of the judgments that I defend are presupposed. I try to limit such presuppositions to those that are necessary for grounding ethical inquiry itself. The basic premise here is that people ought to be treated as independent agents capable of moral responsibility—capable of making moral judgments and guiding their conduct by them. Without this premise, a project such as this one, which aims to establish criteria for ethical judgment, would make little sense.

Ethical inquiry is about making distinctions of the sort that cannot be made by observation of behavior alone. For example, two different people might observe the same classroom, and one might see a fine example of education at work, while the other might condemn the proceedings as indoctrination. How *do* we distinguish between education and indoctrination? Are these just a positive and a negative term for the same thing? Can we distinguish between the government and the mafia? After all, each provides protection at a price. The same sort of question could be asked about socialization and cultural oppression; courtship and seduction; and so on.

I think that these kinds of distinctions can be made, that it is important to make them, and that the differences that ground our ethical judgments can be articulated and defended. In this book, I aim to make ethical distinctions among the various ways in which one form of power is employed.

Acknowledgments

I HAVE INCURRED UNUSUALLY large debts in the course of writing this book, both because the process took quite a long time and because it led me into what, for me, were uncharted waters. I surely would not have made it to shore without the help of the many students and colleagues with whom I shared this project along the way. I can mention only a few of them. For their support, guidance, and challenging criticisms, I would especially like to thank Bradley Bateman, Craig Borowiak, James Bourke, Geoffrey Brennan, Douglas Casson, Peter Euben, Michael Gillespie, Robert Keohane, Alisa Kessel, Thomas Merrill, Michael Munger, Barry Schwartz, David Soskice, Jeremy Sugarman, Richard Weissbourd, Alan Wertheimer, Ruth Zimmerling, and an anonymous reviewer for Princeton University Press.

For the invaluable gift of time, I would like to thank the National Humanities Center, where I held the John E. Sawyer Fellowship, and the Russell Sage Foundation, as well as Duke University's "New Beginnings" seminar. The National Humanities Center also invited me to teach a Dupont Summer Seminar for college teachers on the subject of this book. The seminar contributed greatly to the development of my thoughts.

To Vivien Ravdin, I owe special thanks. With incredible skill, she edited the entire manuscript, and, if you find the prose lively and readable, you have her to thank, too.

My greatest debt is to my husband, Steve, who has been part of this process from beginning to end—reading drafts, commenting, conversing, counseling, and, especially, constantly and enthusiastically encouraging me to see it through to the end. I cannot find adequate words to express my true indebtedness to him.

Portions of this book appeared in three articles: "The Ethics of Incentives: Historical Origins and Contemporary Understandings," *Economics and Philosophy*, 18, copyright © 2002, Cambridge University Press, reprinted with permission; "Ethics in Human Subjects Research: Do Incentives Matter?" coauthored with Jeremy Sugarman, *Journal of Medicine and Philosophy* 29, no. 6, copyright © 2004, reprinted with permission of Taylor and Francis, Inc.; and "Ethics and Incentives: A Political Approach," *American Political Science Review* 100, no. 1 (February), copyright © 2006, American Political Science Association, reprinted with permission of Cambridge University Press.

Strings Attached

Chapter ONE

Why Worry about Incentives?

Express traffic lanes are set aside during rush hour for cars with more than two passengers. A will stipulates that a daughter will inherit only if she agrees to be a stay-at-home mom. West Virginia pays married couples on welfare an extra $100 per month, funded by a federal program to promote marriage. The government authorizes tax deductions for charitable contributions. Companies pay schools to install soda machines or televisions in their lunchrooms. Schools pay students when they get good grades. A prominent economist suggests that the government tax calories in order to reduce obesity. Legislators in South Carolina discuss a proposal to reduce prison sentences for inmates who donate organs. A soup kitchen feeds the homeless only if they attend a church service first. Cities across America offer large tax breaks to entice businesses to relocate. A donor funds college courses on the condition that Ayn Rand's *Atlas Shrugged* is on the reading list. A state legislator suggests paying poor women $1,000 to have their tubes tied while others debate making welfare conditional on the use of the Norplant contraceptive device. All of these are real examples, and the list could be multiplied endlessly.

Increasingly in the modern world, incentives are becoming the tool we reach for when we wish to bring about change. In government, in education, in health care, in private life, and between and within institutions of all sorts, incentives are offered to steer people's choices in certain directions and to bring about desired policy outcomes. So what? you might well ask. Where is the ethical issue here?

From a certain point of view, there is none. Incentives could be viewed as a form of trade. A person is offered something of value to him or her in exchange for doing something valued by the person making the offer. If the offer is accepted, both parties are better off according to their own lights. If that were not the case, and the benefit being offered were not sufficient, the offer would be rejected. This looks like a trade, and a trade is inherently ethical. It is a voluntary transaction that will occur only if both of the parties involved believe that they benefit from it. Thus, trading is free and rational and, for that reason, it can be considered an ethical relation between persons.

Nonetheless, all incentives and disincentives are not alike. We do recognize bribery and blackmail as wrong even though both can be described in neutral terms as situations in which a simple trade takes place: how much is it worth to a customs official to let his duty slide and ignore a smuggling operation? How much is it worth to one person to know that another will not reveal his criminal past?

But are these cases really the same as our trading your two apples for my three oranges? How can we justify distinguishing between legitimate incentives and disincentives on the one hand, and bribery and blackmail on the other? Viewing incentives as simple trades will not get us very far in answering that question.

Moreover, the question is broader than that: there are incentives and disincentives that we might judge illegitimate that nonetheless cannot be classified as bribery or blackmail. The use of incentives in public policy often leaves people with vaguely defined ethical qualms. I expect that some of the examples in the opening paragraph elicited some discomfort in you. What do those "gut reactions" tell us? *Should* some incentives elicit ethical concerns? How do we make sound ethical judgments in the gray areas?

We often meet these issues in everyday life. Some cases are clear. Most people do not object to rush hour express traffic lanes for multi-passenger cars, for example; most people do condemn actions like bribing a judge. But many cases are not so easily agreed upon. In North Carolina, at one time, a licensed driver of high school age could lose that license temporarily if he were failing a course. On hearing of this regulation, my young daughter said, "That's a good idea." My teenage son said, "That's blackmail!"

Examples in the realm of politics are equally controversial. Environmental policies allow companies to buy and sell pollution credits—but does treating pollution as a commodity distort the moral claim that supports its regulation in the first place? The federal government routinely shapes state policies through the use of federal grants in areas it certainly could not constitutionally regulate by federal law—but is this an illegitimate encroachment of power or not? State and local governments offer benefits to businesses to relocate in their area—is this a use of public resources for the public good or an unfair advantage for new businesses? None of these are examples of bribery or blackmail, but all involve the use of incentives in ways that some people find unprincipled and others find perfectly justifiable.

What is the ground of the moral sensibility that so often finds the use of incentives offensive? Some people object, for example, to offering incentives to encourage participation in medical research. In their view, participants ought to be willing volunteers committed to furthering the research enterprise. Otherwise, they are being objectified, used like lab rats for other people's purposes.[1] On the other end of the spectrum of moral sensibilities are those who don't even condemn blackmail. A blackmailer who asks for something in exchange for refraining from revealing an extramarital affair is only threatening to tell the truth, after all. What is wrong with threatening to do something that is perfectly acceptable to do?

The question of the ethics of incentives goes to the heart of a longstanding confrontation between two sorts of moral attitudes. The first might be called the "moralistic attitude," according to which the quality of character of the members of society ought to be a central public concern. Since societies can only function at their best if their members, especially their leaders, are capable of virtues like self-restraint, personal sacrifice, and public responsibility, matters of motivation and character formation are critical for politics. The contrasting view I will call the "economic attitude" or the "Mandevillian attitude." The latter refers to Bernard Mandeville, a Dutch author who famously argued in *The Fable of the Bees* (1714) that private vices often yield public benefits. In this view, our proper concern should be the aggregate outcomes of individual choices and not their motivation or moral quality. The skillful politician is the one who so manages society that even the self-indulgence and vanity of its members produce public goods. The "Mandevillians" scorn the "moralists" as soft-headed and irrational, willing to sacrifice all sorts of beneficial developments on the altar of an illusory project of moral perfection. The "moralists," in turn, condemn the "Mandevillians" as reductionist cynics who destroy, by denying, the higher human possibilities.

It is an argument that goes back a long way and still takes many forms. One can find it today whenever the ethics of incentives arises as an issue. For example, in the debate over whether to offer payment as an incentive for people to give blood, some worry that altruistic motives will disappear once payment becomes accepted practice (which will lead to blood shortages as well). Others question whether a system that relies on altruism can efficiently ensure a sufficient supply of blood.[2]

Controversies like these have been around for a very long time, and there is every reason to believe that they will continue in one form or another. There are two recent versions of "Mandevillian" thinking worthy of note. For the last ten years or so, "conditional cash transfer programs" have been popular in Latin America and the Caribbean and have recently been tried in the United States as well. These are programs where poor mothers are given cash payments on the condition that they get their children vaccinated, or send them to school regularly, or some similar requirement.* The term is new, but the general idea is not. Similarly, there has been much discussion recently of "libertarian paternalism." This approach seeks to change people's behavior by structuring choice situations in certain ways. For example, one can ensure that people will save more for retirement if they are automatically enrolled in a 401k plan and have to make the effort to "opt out" than if they have to make the effort to "opt in."[3] These approaches seek to increase responsible behavior without dealing directly with responsibility as an aspect of character. This "Mandevillian attitude" obviously favors the use of incentives of all kinds, while the "moralists" condemn them. *But neither position gives grounds for making ethical distinctions among incentives themselves.*

I hope to do exactly that by adopting an alternative approach to the question of the ethics of incentives—by looking at incentives as a form of power. The use of incentives is one possible answer to the following question: How can one person get another person to do what he wants him to do? When considering forms of power, the classic alternatives are force and persuasion: people can make you do what they want you to do, or they can convince you to want to do what they want you to do. But bargaining—including incentives—is a third form of power. People

---

*Can you imagine a similar program offering tax breaks to middle-class mothers who keep their teenage children drug-free?

can give you something that you want in exchange for your compliance with what they want. Suppose I want you to do X, and you are reluctant to do it. If I cannot persuade you to do it and I do not have the capability to coerce you to do it, I may still be able to induce you to do X by offering you an incentive. Coercion, persuasion, and bargaining are different forms of power. Each is sometimes legitimate and sometimes not. Examining the standards for the legitimacy of all kinds of power will help clarify the criteria for distinguishing legitimate from illegitimate uses of incentives.

Considering incentives as an exercise of power raises ethical issues that are not brought to light by the typical approach. When incentives are considered exclusively as a type of trade, the crucial ethical question is, "Is this transaction voluntary?"[4] The approach suggested here goes further. It raises many additional ethical questions in considering the use, and abuse, of incentives. It explains why some incentives are generally recognized as problematic despite their formal similarity to other kinds of trades. It takes seriously the ethical impulse behind the discomfort that many people experience in reaction to incentive programs, such as some of those presented at the beginning of this chapter. And, most important, it allows us to establish standards for making crucial ethical distinctions. Different kinds of incentives are not alike in the ethical considerations they raise; if we consider incentives exclusively within an economic framework—as simple trades—these important differences are obscured.

Thinking about incentives as a form of power, along with coercion and persuasion, also brings to light important concerns about democratic politics. We are accustomed to thinking about incentives as an alternative to coercion: economic sanctions, rather than military attack, for example, or pollution credit markets, rather than regulation (sometimes called "command and control"). And incentives certainly seem to have the moral high ground over coercion as an alternative. But coercion is not the only alternative.

Incentives might just as readily be considered in contrast to persuasion. Persuasion, after all, is also a means of exerting power.[5] Incentives attempt to circumvent the need for persuasion by giving people extrinsic reasons to make the choices that the person or institution offering the incentive wishes them to make. When incentives are employed, there is no need to convince people that collective goals are good or to motivate them to pursue those goals by appeals to rational argument, personal conviction, or intrinsic motivations. Experts and powerful elites can thus direct institutions and shape people's choices without the sort of public discussion and consent that ideally characterize democratic processes of decision-making. To take an example close to home: at many colleges and universities, collective bodies of faculty members have a primary role in designing the curriculum. At the same time, individual faculty members often receive incentives from private donors to develop specific kinds of courses. At what point does this practice of private incentives preempt or undercut collective faculty deliberation over educational goals and practices? At what point does the faculty as a collective body lose control over the curriculum? In this case, incentives seem problematic indeed. When the alternative to an incentive is persuasion rather than coercion, the ethical superiority of the use of incentives is not obvious at all.

Yet there is always pressure toward the use of incentives in politics and government. I have drawn examples from all arenas of social interaction, private and public. But the approach taken here is particularly important for politics. Politics—especially in democracies—is at least as much a matter of noncoercive forms of power as it is a matter of coercion. Politicians cannot govern without popular support or the cooperation of coalition partners and allies of all sorts—and that cooperation cannot be compelled. Government must operate with carrots as well as with sticks. The only options besides coercion are bargaining and persuasion, and persuasion is often limited in its effectiveness. This is why some form of bargaining often will be the only effective method available—usually incentives. It is particularly important, then, to understand and articulate the complex ethical issues involved in their use as a tool of government: to recognize that incentives are not necessarily preferable to all forms of coercion; that incentives sometimes substitute for persuasive processes, which is a real cost in a democracy; and that the fact that incentives are voluntary transactions does not settle the ethical questions raised by their use.

It is impossible to address ethical questions without first making them visible. The danger is that once incentives are introduced in certain areas and people become habituated to their use, the important questions simply no longer arise. Consider plea bargaining. There was a time when the courts condemned plea bargaining. Today, nearly 95 percent of felony convictions involve a guilty plea. Plea bargaining can appear to be acceptable because it is a voluntary agreement where both parties seem to be satisfied with the terms of the agreement. But if the criminal justice system is meant to mete out punishment that is deserved, plea bargaining ensures that that goal will never be met. Either innocent people plead guilty falsely or guilty parties receive punishment that is less than they purportedly deserve. The important point here is that today, these are not major issues for general public discussion. Over time, we have moved from consensus around the idea that plea bargaining is illegitimate to tacit acceptance of the practice.[6] I hope that this book will make its readers worry about things they did not worry about before.

Once worried, we need to reach some kind of judgment. This book assesses incentives, along with the various forms of coercion and persuasion, in order to articulate standards for making those judgments. This is the task of chapter 4, and that is where the theoretical heart of the argument can be found. Before embarking on that task, I present, in chapter 2, an historical account of the use of the term "incentives" and of the introduction of incentives in scientific management and behavioral psychology. This history, surprising in many respects, lends considerable support to my approach. "Incentives" came into the language in the early part of the twentieth century in America. During this period, the language of social control and of social engineering was quite prevalent, and incentives were understood to be one tool in the social engineers' toolbox—an instrument of power. Not coincidentally, incentives were also extremely controversial at this time and were criticized from several quarters as dehumanizing, manipulative, heartless, and exploitative. When incentives are viewed as instruments of power, the controversial ethical aspects of their use come readily to the fore.

This history is followed, in chapter 3, by a discussion of the meaning of "incentives." The term has become so ubiquitous that it has almost lost all boundaries and definition. I try here to distinguish incentives both from other forms of motivation and from other forms of trade or exchange, reward or compensation. The discussion allows me to isolate a few core characteristics of the kind of incentives that need to concern us.

Having laid this groundwork, in chapter 4 I suggest three basic standards for distinguishing ethical from unethical uses of incentives. These are legitimacy of purpose, voluntariness, and effect on the character of the parties involved. These standards, in turn, rest on the notion that ethical uses of any kind of power must treat human beings as free and rational agents.

Chapter 5 takes up the problem of making practical judgments: how to apply abstract standards in practice. In addition to evaluating any incentive against the three basic standards, we need to look at its context and alternatives. We will find that there is no "rule of thumb" that can be applied without consideration of the circumstances. One cannot know whether or not it is good to put a cast on someone's leg without knowing first whether or not the leg is broken. Examples from medicine, business, education, government, and so forth show what sorts of questions need to be asked in particular cases. These include the following: Which of the standards is most important in this case? Does the incentive work better than the alternatives? Is it fair? Does the incentive mask accountability? Is this a case of undue influence?

Taking all of these questions into consideration, in chapter 6 I explore in more detail four very different domains where incentives have been controversial: plea bargaining; recruiting medical research subjects; the loan policies of the International Monetary Fund (IMF); and motivating children to learn. Each of these cases illuminates a web of concerns surrounding the ethics of incentives and illustrates how legitimate and illegitimate incentives can be differentiated.

The discussion of plea bargaining explores the contrast between viewing plea bargaining as a contract between two individuals and viewing it as an exercise of state power. The latter perspective focuses attention on whether this practice serves the proper purposes of the criminal justice system: establishing guilt or innocence and appropriately punishing the guilty. I argue that when the state offers leniency in exchange for a guilty plea, it subverts these purposes and acts illegitimately.

The next case is the use of incentives to recruit subjects for medical research. The ethics of this practice has been heavily debated, with critics primarily concerned that large incentives offered to vulnerable populations are coercive, violating the requirement of voluntary consent. I argue that the exclusive focus on voluntariness has limited the discussion. Even though, in my view, these incentives are not coercive, there are other ethical issues that come into play. I conclude that, with some important exceptions, the use of incentives to recruit research subjects is, perhaps surprisingly, benign.

IMF loan conditionality is another area where voluntariness is only one among a number of complex ethical issues. Everyone involved in this debate seems to agree that in order to avoid undue influence, IMF loan conditions must be limited to requirements directly related to the purposes of the fund. But this turns out to be a very difficult line to draw. How far can the IMF go in stipulating national policies and institutional structures—even if these might ensure that the borrowing country will have a strong enough economy to repay its loans and avoid future debt? How effective are IMF loan conditions in practice?

Is it fair for the poor to bear the burden of restoring economic health? And what responsibility does the IMF have when its programs fail?

Finally, I consider the use of incentives to motivate children to learn, particularly recent "pay for grades" programs. Here, we can see that incentives have inherent limitations. In educational settings, they can work for some purposes (e.g., performing routine tasks) but not for others (e.g., problem solving). And their effects tend to be short-lived. Moreover, where children are self-motivated, incentives predictably "backfire," turning play into work and decreasing a child's interest. In evaluating the use of incentives with children, we need to attend to considerations of character as well. How do different types of motivators affect not only learning but also, for example, self-motivation and the sense of mastery? The discussion of this case allows me to distinguish when incentives in education are likely to be useful and when they are likely to be counterproductive.

Examination of these various cases reveals the multiplicity of questions that must be asked before coming to a judgment. And so chapter 7 returns to the contrast between treating incentives simply as a form of trade and treating incentives as a form of power. The problem with the "trade" approach is that it tends to focus on voluntariness as the only important ethical issue to consider. To increase a person's choices always seems to be a good thing, but it does not settle every ethical question. Here I try to show that there are some offers that should not be made, even if a person is perfectly free to reject them.

To take an extreme example, in William Styron's novel *Sophie's Choice*, a Nazi concentration-camp officer offers a woman the opportunity to save the life of one of her two children. If she refuses to choose one, both will die. But the same act of choosing life for one child is also the choice of death for the other. Had the officer actually wished to save the life of a child, he could have made the choice between the two children himself. His decision would have been authoritative, but it would have been far preferable to giving the choice to the mother. In this case, what seems to be a gift of choice is a perfect expression of cruelty.

In less extreme cases, offers can be paternalistic, manipulative, seductive, exploitative, or irresponsible in a wide variety of ways. Hence, I try to take the discussion in this chapter "beyond voluntariness" to include additional ethical standards.

I also consider the contrast between two ways of thinking about what voluntariness itself is: having a choice or acting autonomously. Incentives always present people with choices, but they can be an affront to their autonomy at the same time. This observation explains why incentives predictably backfire in certain situations.

Finally, in chapter 8, I raise the broader question of the relation between incentives and democratic politics. This question arises first in the historical investigation of chapter 2. During the Progressive era, incentives were considered a tool of social engineering, and social engineering was hotly contested. Is social engineering democratic or anti-democratic? The use of incentives as a tool of government policy appears to increase our choices and protect a space of freedom. We can always refuse the offer. This seems to be better than government regulations that foreclose options and establish penalties for transgressions. But, to the extent that incentives are one of the ways in which experts seek to manipulate behavior and to the extent that incentive systems substitute for persuasion and foreclose deliberation and debate, a democratic people ought to be deeply suspicious of them. At the very least, the question of the ethics of incentives leads directly to the question of the role of experts in a democracy and finally, further still, to the question of what kind of citizens we aspire to be.

My first aim in this book is to make visible the problematic ethical issues involved in the use of incentives. It is impossible to do that without uncovering a host of other issues as well. My second aim is to find ways to distinguish legitimate from illegitimate incentives. That also proves to be a complicated matter. We encounter incentives frequently in daily life and are called upon to make judgments about them. We often make those judgments with relative ease. But if you scratch the surface of the matter, you will soon find yourself thinking about psychology and ethics, democracy and expertise, power and freedom.

Chapter TWO

Incentives Then and Now

The Clock and the Engineer

WHY BEGIN WITH history? What can be learned from the story of the origins of "incentives talk"? In this case, the historical story is illuminating because it challenges contemporary misconceptions (1) that incentives are identical to market mechanisms; (2) that they are, therefore, alternatives to social and political control; and (3) that they have always been largely uncontroversial. Assuming these propositions are true, it is no wonder that incentives tend to get an ethical "pass" and are accepted without a great deal of scrutiny. But none of these notions could be further from the truth. On the contrary, the history of the origins of the concept of incentives highlights the extent to which incentives were originally understood in contrast to the automatic forces of the market; and it clearly identifies incentives as instruments of social control, deeply implicated in ethical and political controversy from their inception.

Origins

For more than 250 years, starting in about 1600, the word "incentive" meant "inciting or arousing to feeling or action, provocative, exciting." Uses cited by the authoritative *Oxford English Dictionary* include: "The Lord Shaftesbury . . . made an incentive speech in the House of Lords (1734)," or "This Paper is principally designed as an incentive to the Love of our Country (1713)." The last example cited of the term in this sense is dated 1866 and, like the others, it comes from an English source. Then there is a striking change. "Mr. Charles E. Wilson . . . is urging war industries to adopt 'incentive pay'—that is, to pay workers more if they produce more." This is the first example from the same dictionary of the use of the term in its contemporary sense, and it is an American example dated three quarters of a century later in 1943.

There is a huge gap in time, place, and meaning between the two sorts of citations, a gap that introduces several puzzles. What was happening in America when the new meaning of incentives was introduced? Why is this conception missing from the vocabulary in the seventeenth and eighteenth centuries, the very years in which the idea of a market economy was being discovered and articulated? We are accustomed to believe that our thinking about political economy rests on the work of the likes of John Locke, Bernard Mandeville, Adam Smith, David Hume, Jeremy Bentham, James Mill, John Stuart Mill, and the authors of *The Federalist Papers*. But with very few exceptions, "incentive" does not appear in *any* of their writings.

Of course, one might argue that so long as the conceptions are there, it matters little whether the term is not. One can find discussions in eighteenth- and early nineteenth-century writings of how what we now call incentives might work to motivate people, how institutions can be arranged so as to encourage particular behaviors, and so forth. For that matter, in ancient societies, there were certainly practices we would describe today as incentive systems. It does not seem that the use of incentives is new. So what does it matter if the term is relatively new?

If a term has changed, are we really dealing with precisely the same idea? A change in terminology can indicate a change in perspective. Whereas our forebears spoke of engaging people's interests and motivating, inducing, enticing, or encouraging people to act in certain ways, we speak of using incentives to prompt particular actions. The different expressions do not quite say or connote the same things. The task is to discover the distinctive character given to today's concept of incentives by the historical setting in which the term "incentives" emerged.

That setting was early twentieth-century America, where the term appeared in three different areas at about the same time. The first of these was the new field of scientific management of industry. Here, "incentives" referred to piece-rate, bonus, or premium wage systems. The second area was the burgeoning debate over the practicality of socialist economics: would workers have an "incentive" to work if they could not be rewarded according to their effort? In this discussion, the term was usually used broadly, as synonymous with motivation generally. Lastly, the term appeared in the developing field of behavioral psychology. In this field, the term expressed a particular kind of motivation—an extrinsic prompt, deliberately designed to elicit a desired behavior that will shift behavior from its usual paths.

Incentives became an issue in all three areas as experts perceived that the automatic forces driving behavior were failing—when market wages were not eliciting maximum production, for example, or, for the behavioral psychologists, when the automatic workings of instinct no longer seemed to direct behavior and settled habits were seen as maladaptive. In all these cases, there seemed to be a need to supplement (or counteract) the usual, automatic forces in order to bring about progressive social change. This is what incentives were designed to do.

Prevailing conceptions of social planning and control in the early decades of the twentieth century in America formed the context for the introduction of "incentives," and it is no accident that the term "social control" was introduced at about the same time.[1] The idea can be expressed best, perhaps, by a fundamental shift in metaphor. Throughout the seventeenth and eighteenth centuries in British social philosophy, the dominant metaphor is the clock. Society is conceived as a huge and intricate clockwork that functions automatically and predictably once it has been set in motion. The whole system is governed by mechanical laws that organize the relations of each part. Just as Newton discovered the laws of gravity that govern motion in the natural world, Adam Smith discovered the laws of supply and demand that govern the motion of the economy. Smith used the metaphor of the watch and the machine in describing social systems.[2]

Now contrast the clock metaphor with the metaphorical persona of the "social engineer," and you will begin to see the distance between America in the Progressive era and British thought of the previous centuries. Adam Smith's "invisible hand" becomes very visible indeed. Smith himself criticized people who thought that society could be regulated as if one were moving men on a chessboard.[3] But in America at the turn of the twentieth century, many people believed that social relations could be ordered and arranged through deliberate interventions by those with scientific expertise. In this view, society is not a smoothly functioning, orderly mechanism but an amalgam of forces in constant flux that can be directed to bring about progress.[4] Organisms adapt to their environment; thus, engineering the environment can help bring about successful adaptations. Frederick Taylor, the founder of scientific management in industry, wrote: "There is a close analogy between the methods of modern engineering and this type of management."[5] This is the context within which the term "incentives" was introduced and within which the meaning of incentives can be understood: incentive systems are one of the tools in the social engineer's toolbox.

In 1911, Frederick Taylor published *The Principles of Scientific Management*, outlining his system of factory production and its rationale.[6] Taylor's system was devised to combat the widespread practice of "soldiering," or deliberate underproduction by workers on the shop floor. According to Taylor, this practice had become a "fixed habit" because workers were convinced that more efficient production would yield greater profits for the owners but layoffs for them. The best management practice for dealing with this problem hitherto, Taylor believed, had been "initiative and incentive" management, which was designed to spur greater production by offering additional rewards for individual workers who increased their output. But he argued forcefully that these practices would prove effective only if joined to his new idea of scientific time-study and task management.

Taylor proposed to create a class of managers in the factory who would employ scientific analyses to determine precisely the amount of time required to complete each element of the production process, to divide tasks in a rational manner, and to communicate to each worker precise expectations for the tasks he should accomplish and the amount of time allotted for each task. The entire scheme "has for its very foundation the firm conviction that the true interests of the two [employers and employees] are one and the same; that prosperity for the employer . . . cannot exist unless it is accompanied by prosperity for the employee."[7]

In short, Taylor's scientific management was to be the solution to the following problem: how to get people to act in accordance with their *true* interests, when their settled habits tend in the opposite direction. Experts who understand what those interests are and possess scientific knowledge of the right techniques (incentives among them) can engineer a situation to get people to move in the right direction.

Elton Mayo, though less well-known than Taylor, was another major figure in the development of scientific management in the 1930s. He shared Taylor's view of the fundamental problem in industrial relations. Nineteenth-century work habits, appropriate for a period of individualized production, were maladaptive in the industrial age, which required a much higher degree of social cooperation in the factory unit. As a psychologist, Mayo had begun his working life treating World War I veterans, and, in his writings, he made explicit analogies between the problems of social cooperation, stress, fatigue, and maladjustment in army units and factory units. He saw that defective factory organization and personnel policies could create similar worker stress and hinder cooperation between workers and management. For Mayo, labor unrest was not a matter of any fundamental conflict of class interests but could be understood better as the product of maladjustment in the workforce. The personnel counseling interview was a key technique for bringing the individual worker to a proper understanding of his situation and relieving feelings that could lead to conflict. Properly engineered factory systems run by trained and psychologically sophisticated management experts could bring about the kind of social cooperation required for modern industrial democracies to function.[8] Thus, for both Mayo and Taylor, incentives were one technique among many in a much broader program of progressive social engineering for American industry.

The development of scientific management was embedded in political and moral controversy from the beginning. The attempt to secure social cooperation in industry took place against the background of considerable labor unrest, and, not surprisingly, American unions did not look with favor upon Taylorism. In 1911, the introduction of "time-study" techniques provoked a strike that led to a congressional investigation of Taylorism.[9] In 1915, Congress forbade the employment of the stopwatch in army workshops.[10]

The scientific claims and academic character of the new management science did not imply, as we might expect today, any sort of claim to ethical neutrality or apolitical objectivity. Both the adherents of scientific management and its detractors understood it in moral and political terms.

To some of its adherents, scientific management and the value it placed on efficiency promised to promote the Christian virtues of hard work, thrift, and will power while checking the greed of employers and the laziness of employees.[11] Taylor wrote in inspirational tones that scientific management would enhance peace, prosperity, and happiness.[12] Wallace Donham, dean of the Harvard Business School, as well as Elton Mayo, defended the new science not only in terms of the immediate benefits it might bring but in terms of its importance for the preservation of Western civilization altogether.[13] Louis Brandeis believed that scientific management would enhance self-respect among workers, decrease class divisions, and improve democracy.[14]

Others, of course, saw in scientific management a heartless system for the dominance, exploitation, and dehumanization of the common man.[15] Charlie Chaplin's 1936 film *Modern Times* brilliantly satirized the tyranny of Taylorite time and task management systems and their tendency to reduce workers to the level of machines.

Incentive wage systems were particularly controversial. For the American labor movement, incentive pay was a major source of complaint, not least because it pitted individual workers against one another and seemed to undermine the professed aim of the new science: fostering cooperation in industry. It wasn't until 1925 that the American Federation of Labor began to make its peace with scientific management. But even then, while it had gradually dropped its objections to various aspects of Taylor's system, it still condemned incentive pay schemes.[16]

In short, "incentives" came into the language of American industry in an atmosphere of heated moral and political controversy. Incentives were offered by people with power to people without it, and everybody knew that. This was an era when people spoke quite unabashedly of the need for government by experts and for behavioral and social engineering, as well as of the need to establish social control. And these were hotly contested matters. The tone of this public discourse is a bit shocking to contemporary ears; today, we tend to take incentives for granted, almost as if they were natural features of our social and political environment.[17] And so conversely, I cannot help but wonder how surprising it would be to Americans in the first decades of the twentieth century to find that, one hundred years later, incentives are generally considered uncontroversial. The ethical and political aspects of incentive mechanisms could not have been more obvious to them.

The second major discourse in which "incentives" made its appearance on the scene is the debate over whether socialist economics would work. In a capitalist economy, the profit motive is supposed to operate automatically to bring about productive labor and productive investment. But in a planned economy, with common ownership, critics asked, "What will take the place of profit as a motivator? Without the profit motive, what 'incentives' will there be for production and investment?" Moreover, if workers are not compensated in proportion to their effort, what will motivate them to work hard? The question of whether or not socialist economies could solve these problems was central to the controversy over socialism in America.[18]

Others who were engaged in the debate over socialism framed the central question quite differently. Incentives are not the crucial issue. In Nobel Prize–winning economist Friedrich A. Hayek's view, the question of motivation is a question of morality and psychology. Thus, it is not an "economic problem"; it is a problem "of an engineering character."[19] The language in which Hayek defined the problem is telling: economics, science, and market forces on one hand; engineering, technology, and incentives on the other. For Hayek, fellow economist Ludwig von Mises, and others, the problem of socialist economics is to determine value in the absence of a pricing system, not to motivate men in the absence of the profit motive.[20] This latter problem was dismissed by Hayek as a problem of social engineering.

In contrast to human agency in planning or engineering, Hayek stressed that the competitive market system operates "although the decision is not consciously made by anybody";[21] "it is not necessary for the working of this system that anybody understand it."[22] This is the metaphor of the clock speaking. Opponents of capitalism, on the other hand, advocated planning because they believed that the automatic economic forces of competition were no longer supplying solutions for modern societies. Hayek provides the following characterization of the temper of the times:

> For more than half a century, the belief that deliberate regulation of all social affairs must necessarily be more successful than the apparent haphazard interplay of independent individuals has continuously gained ground until today there is hardly a political group anywhere in the world which does not want central direction of most human activities in the service of one aim or another. It seemed so easy to improve upon the institutions of a free society which had come more and more to be considered as the result of mere accident, the product of a peculiar historical growth which might as well have taken a different direction. To bring order to such a chaos, to apply human reason to the organization of society, and to shape it deliberately in every detail according to human wishes and the common ideas of justice seemed the only course of action worthy of a reasonable being.[23]

Society was no longer seen as an orderly, clocklike mechanism. The new advocates of social control believed that planning was necessary because of the failure or absence of automatic processes that could rationally order human activities. This is the context in which the concept of incentives becomes salient.

A similar logic undergirded the field of behavioral psychology, which emerged in precisely the same period and within the same general context—but here it is the inefficacy of automatic forces of instinct that is crucial. If instincts are not driving behavior, there must be some kind of external motivators, or incentives, that explain behavior. The term "behaviorism" was coined by John Broadus Watson in an article published in 1913.[24] Watson advocated a new science of psychology that would focus exclusively on observable human behavior rather than on the unobservable (and in his view mythic) phenomena of consciousness.

Behavior was conceived as the organism's attempt to adapt to its environment. And because, to Watson and others, this process of adaptation was not governed by internal forces of instinct, the questions of behavioral research necessarily focused on motivation and learning: "[M]ost of the things we see the adult doing are learned. We used to think that a lot of them were instinctive, that is 'unlearned.' But we are now almost at the point of throwing away the word 'instinct.'"[25]

Watson adopted a version of stimulus-response theory, influenced by the work of Pavlov, to explain behavior. Adjustment or adaptation came to mean the state in which an organism has moved or altered its condition so that the stimulus no longer calls forth a response.[26] The individual is seen as passive, responding rather than initiating behavior, and entirely reactive to external stimuli—and therefore almost infinitely malleable. This left wide room for the scientists to intervene: "The interest of the behaviorist in man's doings is more than the interest of the spectator," wrote Watson. "*[H]e wants to control men's reactions* as physical scientists want to control and manipulate other natural phenomena."[27]

The aim of these efforts at social control is adjustment or adaptation, so the scientist's task is essentially technical—devising the means to accomplish social purposes that themselves are not questioned: "It is presumably not the function of the behaviorist to discuss whether these things which society prescribes serve as a help or a hindrance to the growth or adjustment of the individual. The behaviorist is working under the mandates of society." Arrangement of the proper stimuli could serve to condition children and adults to behave in these socially desirable ways habitually because all behavior is essentially a process of adaptation to the environment.[28]

Following Watson, behavioral psychologists expanded the research into motivation and learning, devising increasingly sophisticated experiments with animal responses to controlled stimuli.[29] B. F. Skinner, Watson's most influential intellectual heir, developed the theory of "operant conditioning" according to which animals, and people, learned to behave in certain ways in response to positive reinforcement of those behaviors. As the field developed, psychologists were interested in understanding how incentives could be used to promote learning, and the term "incentive motivation" was introduced with a technical sense to distinguish certain kinds of motivational processes from others.[30] Experiments moved from simple maze trials with rats, through the use of tokens with chimpanzees, to the use of tokens to teach mental patients simple tasks, to similar efforts with healthy children by the 1960s.[31] But, on the basis of behavioral theories of learning, it is not always easy to distinguish education from manipulation or children from chimpanzees, and, not surprisingly, the ethical implications of behavioral psychology were controversial.

As was the case with scientific management, defenders of behavioral psychology made ethical claims in its favor. Watson, despite the apparent neutrality of his depiction of the behaviorist as a technician serving "the mandates of society," goes on to claim that "some time we will have a behavioristic ethics, experimental in type, which will tell us whether it is advisable from the standpoint of past and future adjustments of the individual to have one wife or many wives; capital punishment or punishment of any kind . . . whether any of our other prescribed courses of conduct make for adjustment of the individual or the contrary."[32] And he closes with a stirring call for a saner world made possible by a scientific approach to human psychology that would liberate people from the bonds of superstition, irrational customs, and unfounded myths.

Behavioral psychology presumed that habits, instincts, and other automatic forces would impose very little constraint on the possibilities for social control. In 1948, Skinner wrote *Walden Two* to suggest the liberating potential of behavioral engineering. Even earlier, Watson became famous for his admittedly exaggerated claim: "Give me a dozen healthy infants, well-formed, and my own special world to bring them up in and I'll guarantee to take any one at random and train him to become any type of specialist I might select—doctor, lawyer, artist . . . even beggarman and thief, regardless of his talents, penchants, tendencies."[33]

Where Watson and Skinner saw tremendous potential for progress and liberation, others saw manipulation and even totalitarianism.[34] Skinner himself provides an interesting list of the common, persistent, and in his view unjustifiable criticisms of behaviorism including the following: it "dehumanizes man"; it is incompatible with "love for one's fellow men"; it is "necessarily antidemocratic because the relation between experimenter and subject is manipulative"; and so forth.[35] Many of these criticisms are strikingly similar to criticisms leveled by workers at the new system of scientific management.[36]

The mechanical view of individual human behavior developed by behavioral psychologists meshes well with the engineering approach to social organization. As we have seen, scientific management, certain critics of socialism, and behavioral psychology all share the presupposition that incentives are the only kind of motivation. The question is not whether to employ them but only how best to employ them to produce social benefits.[37] Not surprisingly, this basic perspective forms the context for the contemporary conception of incentives. Individuals will react in predictable ways to adapt to external stimuli in their environment. Experts who understand the processes of motivation can design incentive mechanisms to alter the environment so as to direct individual behavior toward desired social goals. In particular, various forms of social cooperation that would not emerge automatically can be fostered through social engineering. There is no assumption here that the rational ordering of human behavior could be spontaneously produced by self-regulating forces. There is no sense that there are laws of social organization that constrain expert efforts at control, such as the laws of an economic market.

Thus, originally, the concept of incentives was embedded not in the framework of an "Adam Smith"–type explanation of economic laws but in the very different set of ideas associated with the engineering paradigm. This paradigm raised new questions about both the status of individual freedom and individual purpose, and the use and abuse of expertise and social control. These controversies over the ethical implications of behavioral psychology and scientific management inevitably involved the central question for this study: understanding that incentives are a means of controlling the behavior of others, how can we distinguish legitimate from illegitimate uses of them?

The Clock and the Engineer

Let us pause to consider what the historical inquiry tells us. The observation that the term "incentives" does not appear in its contemporary sense until the early twentieth century in America indicates that there is a distinctively American contribution to the very idea of incentives. In particular, there is a distinctively American psychology that supports this idea. While it is undeniable that European thought has always been influential in America, this idea is not a European import.[38]

To tell the full story would require exploring the American intellectual roots of the "worldview" of the Progressive era, with its valorization of efficiency, expertise, and, above all, social planning. This was the setting for the birth of the social science disciplines of economics, sociology, political science, and psychology, and these disciplines were intimately linked with one another at their inception.[39]

This was also a time when Americans were impressed with the idea that they were living in a new age. The second industrial revolution and developments in science and technology had created a world to which traditional modes of behavior no longer seemed suited. The shocking experience of World War I as a war like none other intensified the feeling that new adaptations were required for the modern world. How could human behavior be redirected to accommodate modern conditions? What could modern science teach us about the possibilities for human progress? Such questions required a reassessment of the psychology of individual motivation, and it is certainly not surprising to find a conception like "incentives" becoming prevalent in several different kinds of conversations throughout the interwar period. These conversations took place within the context of a powerful optimism among those who advocated social control, scientific planning, and behavioral engineering—an optimism that in some quarters even survived World War II but one that seems utterly incredible today.[40]

Behavioral engineering and social control became legitimate objectives against the background of the era's rapid economic and political change. As social scientists, economic experts, and national policymakers saw it, any sort of social progress would require individuals to adapt to an ever-changing environment—and in particular, to one in which the changes brought about by rapid industrialization seemed radical. The social world had come to look something like Darwin's natural world, one of change and contingency where people were either "well-adjusted" or "maladjusted" to their social environment. To manage change and contingency in such a way as to serve the collective good required expertise and planning.[41]

I return to the clock and the engineer as metaphors for social organization to make the point a little differently. Both are "machine images," but there is a crucial difference between them. The seventeenth- and eighteenth-century image of the clock implies inertial motion, an idea reflected, for example, in Thomas Hobbes's statements that there is no life where there is no desire or that life is a ceaseless seeking after power.[42] The natural state of things is to be in perpetual motion. The twentieth-century image of social engineering implies inertial rest. Without the active interposition of the engineer, without the particular incentive, there would be no motion or motivation.[43] Things move only when prompted. Incentives are required to set the wheels turning, to build and to progress.

And there is considerable scope for human design when the natural world is no longer conceived as a clocklike mechanism designed by a divine "watchmaker." The human engineer works in a world where society is understood in terms of mutability and adaptation in a dynamic interaction of individual and environment. In contrast, the orderly, clocklike mechanism of the seventeenth-century world exhibits the rationality of its maker. The natural "clock" is initially wound by God and then continues its perpetual, repetitive, necessary, and intelligible motion.

John Winthrop, in his famous sermon delivered aboard the *Arabella* in 1630, speaks of the workings of mercy in the soul through the metaphor of a clock:

> when wee bid one make the clocke strike he doth not lay hand on the hammer which is the immediate instrument of the sound but setts on worke the first mover or maine-wheele, knoweing that will certainely produce the sound which hee intends; soe the way to drawe men to the workes of mercy is not by force of Argument from the goodness or necessity of the worke, for though this course may enforce a rationallminde to some present Act of mercy as is frequent in experience, yet it cannot worke such a habit in a Soule as shall make it prompt upon all occasions to produce the same effect but by frameing these affeccions of love in the hearte which will as natively bring forth the other, as any cause doth produce the effect.[44]

The habits of the soul are like the workings of the clock, automatically and regularly producing the desired effects. In Winthrop's view, to rely on rational argument for motivation would be like having to work the clock's hammer from the outside, individually, each time. Incentives are rather like rational argument in this respect; unlike habits, incentives are discrete external prompts that need to be offered repeatedly or continuously to elicit particular behaviors.[45] And, as we have seen, the term emerged in the vocabulary at a time when traditional habits, as well as other automatic forces of instinct or of the market, were thought to serve the needs of society no longer.

Ethical and Political Controversies

The historical inquiry also reveals that incentives can be viewed from an entirely different ethical and political perspective than the one to which we are accustomed. There is a remarkable contrast: today, talk of incentives is generally considered innocuous; when the term first came into general use, incentives were highly controversial. Incentives are only necessary to move people to do what they would otherwise *not* want to do (either because there are no good reasons inherent in the situation to do it or because they do not understand those reasons and it would be too costly or ineffective to try to persuade people of them). Within the frameworks of scientific management and behavioral psychology, incentives were understood as instruments in the hands of powerful experts, useful for managing and directing people's behavior to achieve certain social purposes. The possibilities for abuse were obvious, and the very legitimacy of incentive systems altogether was an open question. Incentives were often seen as an inherently suspect form of manipulation and control.

Moreover, these discussions took place in a period when the tensions between democracy and technocracy, closely associated with class tensions, were at the center of political discourse. Originally, the technocratic use of incentives was criticized by some as manipulative and elitist. It was defended by others who wished to empower experts in order to ensure social progress and viewed expert opinion as an improvement over democratic discussion.[46] Today, we rarely think of incentives as an alternative to democracy. Instead, incentives are assimilated to market mechanisms and viewed as a favorable alternative to state coercion. But it is well to remember that they are also an alternative to persuasion or democratic deliberation in influencing people's choices.

In addition to these political questions, the mechanical view of human motivation and choice implied by the use of incentives raised ethical issues as well. How is human freedom to be understood if individual choice is reduced to the response to external stimuli? If our choices are guided by incentives of one sort or another, can any choice be said to be morally better than any other? What is the place of traditional norms or of socialization to certain habits of character if they can be easily altered by the impact of particular incentives at any moment? Does character have any meaning at all? How is our humanity to be understood in the machine age?[47] These sorts of questions were clearly implicated in the conversations within which "incentives" became an operative modern term.

In America in the early part of the twentieth century, incentives represented a break with earlier modes of thought and were understood in many instances as a corrective response to the deficiencies of automatic market forces. Particularly in the context of industrial relations, incentives were understood as a tool employed by elite experts in implementing projects of social control. In this context, the use of incentives raised clear and controversial ethical and political issues. Today the situation is altogether different. Incentives are widely employed throughout all kinds of social and governmental institutions without creating great controversy. Moreover, the term "incentive" has become abstracted from the ethical and political issues in which it was once embedded. It is a term that has come to be used broadly and indiscriminately, so much so that it now often includes market forces, even though it was originally employed in contradistinction to the market, as we have seen.

Sensitivity to the history just canvassed should help clarify the meaning of "incentives," as well as highlight the ethical issues involved with their use. What, specifically, do we mean by "incentives" today? And why have they largely ceased to provoke ethical and political controversy? We turn now to consider the meaning of incentives, hoping to recover or uncover the distinctions between this term and related concepts, as well as to identify the hidden assumptions behind the idea.

Chapter THREE

"Incentives Talk": What Are Incentives Anyway?

What are incentives? This obvious initial question turns out to be quite a bit more difficult to answer than one might expect. The term has a variety of meanings and usages, some in ordinary language and some in the technical vocabulary of academic disciplines such as psychology and economics. Most important, "incentive" is used so widely and indiscriminately today that the boundaries of the concept are blurred. It is used to refer to virtually every kind of motivation at the same time that it is used to refer to virtually every kind of exchange or choice situation. Consequently, important distinctions are lost, and the presuppositions embedded in the concept of "incentives" come to affect our thinking about phenomena that are really quite disparate.

For example, many people use the term "incentive" as the equivalent of "motivation." But this use of the term implies that motivation works in the manner described by behavioral psychologists: an external stimulus produces a response, as the smell of cheese stimulates a mouse to navigate a maze. The danger is that all motivation will come to be conceived this way.

Similarly, when "incentive" is used very broadly—to describe both market forces and behavior-inducing social policies—the distinction is lost between cooperative exchanges and bargains involving the exercise of power. The danger is that all sorts of bargains will come to seem equally benign.

One way to begin to explore what incentives are is to ask what the term "incentives" is *for*. What work does it do that cannot be done by associated terms? In chapter 2, I considered historically why the term became useful when it did. I turn now to consider analytically what this term expresses that is distinctive and cannot be adequately captured by other vocabulary. Despite its current quite general usage, a distinctive specific meaning of the term remains. One approach to isolating this distinctive meaning is to identify situations where only the word "incentive" will do and to distinguish them from situations where another would do equally well or better. Distinguishing incentives from habituation, from rewards, from wages, and from other related ideas is one means of establishing the boundaries of the conception. The result is more precision, as the concept is given "definition" in the sense of form or outline without loss of richness and context.

Recovering this core meaning of "incentives" should highlight distinctions between the many kinds of motivation and motivating factors involved when people make choices. My hope is that understanding the contemporary meaning of incentives and its presuppositions will help explain why incentives are so uncontroversial now as compared to the early twentieth century. Why are the ethical issues so easily overlooked?

Incentives and Motivation

Recall how the term "incentive" altered in meaning over time. A word that first meant "arousing passionate feeling or action" has come to refer to a factor involved in the rational calculation of one's interests.[1] How does the contemporary usage of the term "incentives" affect how we understand the related psychological concepts of reason, passion, and motivation? And what does that understanding imply, in turn, about the politics and the ethics of the use of incentives?

"Incentive" is sometimes used as if it were synonymous with "motivation" generally. There is even a new verb form of the noun that has recently entered the language, "incentivize," by which we mean "to motivate." But there are several important sorts of motivation that are not suggested by the term. Would it make sense to say that a person's sense of responsibility was the "incentive" that led her to care for her aging mother? Is curiosity the "incentive" that leads a child to dig a hole in the backyard? Compare "President Obama incentivized African American children to pursue political careers" to "President Obama inspired African American children to pursue political careers."

There are many kinds of motivation. When the term "incentive" or "incentivize" is used as if it encompassed all forms of motivation, we implicitly deny this variety. The term obscures phenomena like habitual behavior, action motivated by a sense of responsibility or curiosity, or the inspiration of a role model or an ideal.

In general, any action that is initiated by the individual, or understood as internally motivated, is not easily incorporated into the concept of incentive. Incentives are external prompts to which the individual responds. Individuals are assumed to be passive and to act in response to incentives in their environment. But human agency is much more complicated than that. An incentive is one particular kind of motivation, a subset of the more general category. To use "incentive" as a synonym for "motivation" is to radically narrow our understanding of the psychology of human action.[2]

Today, if someone says, "I have no incentive to get up in the morning," he might mean either "I have no reason to get up in the morning" or "I have no desire to get up in the morning." Each of these statements suggests a state of mind and a problem quite different from the other. In the first case, one might respond by trying to find the speaker something to do. In the second case, one might consider treatment for depression. Yet the loose use of the term "incentive" to apply to both cases renders the distinction between them a "distinction without a difference."

This is not a trivial matter. The difference between reason and desire is a difference that has long been considered critically important for judging the ethics of choice as well as the freedom involved in choosing. According to some understandings of human freedom, it makes no sense to speak of a response to desire or passion as a voluntary act.[3] The root of "passion" is "pathos": to suffer, to be acted upon. It is related to "passive" and "patient" as opposed to "active" and "agent." To respond automatically to the promptings of the passions is to be their "slave" or to act out of necessity. Freedom, on the other hand, implies the capacity for self-control: the ability to resist impulse and to guide one's choices according to reason. According to this view, rationality is the ground for the possibility of ethical behavior altogether.

But the concept of incentives, particularly as it is used in contemporary economic thought, is embedded in a theory of choice that does not rely on the distinction between reason and desire and the potential for conflict between them.[4] In this view, choices are determined by the interaction of individual preferences with the constraints of a particular situation (including incentives and disincentives broadly construed). Preferences are neither reasons nor desires. And to judge among preferences according to an independent rational standard forms no part of this sort of economic analysis. Instead, reason is simply the faculty that allows us to calculate how best to attain what we prefer. As such, we cannot make a "rational" judgment that one preference is in any way better than another.*

---

*This is axiomatic in contemporary economic thought, and it is the most striking departure from the classical political economy of the eighteenth century. Other axioms are shared: that interest is the most reliable motivator of human action; that individuals are generally the best judges of their own interests; that people make choices so as to improve their condition. But in the

This manner of thinking makes it very difficult to recognize incentives that might properly be called "temptations." If rationality is to choose according to your preferences, then irrationality is to choose contrary to your preferences. But "to choose contrary to your preferences" is, in many instances, synonymous with "virtue" (particularly the virtue of moderation). Anyone who has ever resisted a piece of chocolate cake knows this. To choose contrary to your preferences is virtuous whenever it is rational to resist your desires. But such a conclusion can only be reached if some "preferences" can be judged—rationally—to be ethically superior to others.[5] These ethical issues are difficult to see when the language of "incentives" and "preferences" collapses the distinctions between reason and passion, judgment and desire.

In order to address the ethical issues, we need to have a language that allows us to distinguish between different kinds of motivation. In economic thinking, an incentive is meant to alter the balance of the costs and benefits of a particular choice so as to alter a person's course of action: all choices are made for essentially the same reason, to maximize utility. But if all action is motivated by the desire to maximize utility, ethical questions that depend on distinguishing some kinds of motivating intentions from others will not be asked.[6]

I have already highlighted the need to acknowledge intrinsic, or internal, forms of motivation. It is also important to know whether someone acted for love or money, or whether someone acted to fulfill the goals of a common enterprise or for private gain. At the very least, this information is important for predicting future behavior and for assessing a person's trustworthiness. For example, a person who sometimes does the wrong thing for the right reason might be more trustworthy than the one

---

eighteenth century, the distinction is always made between one's true interests and merely apparent interests; people make mistakes about their interests; interests are not identical to preferences; and neither is identical to duties.

who occasionally does the right thing but for the wrong reason. This information is critical for making ethical judgments, which often involve considering why a person did what she did and whether she did it for the right reason. In contrast, conceiving incentives as the sole mechanism of motivation presupposes that the choices people make are made for the sake of gain or advantage, however broadly understood, and further questions concerning motivation tend to go unasked.

In attempting to recover a particular idea of "incentives" as one kind of motivation only, it is helpful to distinguish them from "rewards" and "punishments" as well. And here, too, making the distinction brings important ethical issues into view, in this case, issues concerning fairness and merit. "Incentive" is often used as if it were a synonym for "reward"[7] and "disincentive" as if it were a synonym for "punishment." But there are significant differences between them. It is always understood that a reward or punishment, unlike an incentive or disincentive, ought to be merited or deserved. Though offering a reward may function as a motivator to action, or as an incentive in that sense, rewards do not always function in this way. For example, people are sometimes rewarded unexpectedly for past achievements. They deserve the reward, but, since they did not anticipate it, it does not serve as a motivator.[8] Similar observations apply to the difference between punishment and disincentives. It is true that punishment or the threat of punishment can have a deterrent effect and thereby function as a disincentive. But many disincentives are not punishments. For example, parking meters are a disincentive for driving downtown but not a punishment for doing so. And punishment may be deserved and justly administered even when it is ineffective as a deterrent.*

---

*Some might argue to the contrary that punishment is only justified where it is effective as a disincentive. But the possibility of the argument underscores the point that punishment and disincentives are not identical.

That the same benefit may be at once deserved, like a reward, and a motivator, like an incentive, is one reason that people tend to identify wages with incentives. But thinking through the distinction between them is instructive. Though wages certainly can function as motivators, they are also compensation. Compensation means "rendering equal," a "recompense or equivalent," "payment for value received or service rendered," or something that "makes up for a loss" (as in the term "unemployment compensation"). There are other forms of compensation in addition to wages. Compensation renders an equivalent for losses sustained in a given situation, such as injuries sustained in an accident. Reimbursement compensates for the costs a person might incur, for example, in traveling to and from a business meeting. Wages provide an equivalent or compensation for effort expended or services received. Compensation and incentives are by no means identical. For example, the per diem received for jury service in the United States, where citizens are required to serve on juries, is a clear case of compensation that is not an incentive because it is not a motivator.

Compensation in all of its forms equalizes or redresses a balance, and so, to speak of "fair compensation," "fair reimbursement," or "fair wages" is entirely sensible. But to speak of a "fair incentive" is not sensible because incentives are not a form of compensation. Instead, an incentive is a benefit (which need not be monetary) designed as a motive or inducement to action. The "right" amount for an incentive is the amount it takes to elicit the desired response. For example, a bonus is an economic incentive offered to an employee usually designed to motivate the employee to produce beyond the usual expectation but sometimes designed simply to retain the employee's services or to achieve some other objective. The bonus will be the correct amount if it accomplishes its goal efficiently. It cannot be either a fair or an unfair amount, since there is no corresponding loss or expenditure for which it is meant to compensate. This is why people who defend large retention bonuses for corporate executives and people who criticize them "talk past each other." The former see the money as an incentive, while the latter are concerned with equity. They assume that people should in some way earn, merit, or deserve their monetary compensation on the job.

Similarly, when cities offer lucrative incentive packages to attract businesses to relocate in their area, other local businesses are likely to raise a question of fairness. Why does the new company deserve benefits that are unavailable to existing local companies? If the benefits are viewed strictly as incentives, the question of fairness simply doesn't arise.

Generally speaking, the effect of this language of incentives is to render ethical problems less visible. Implicit in how we talk about incentives are a number of other understandings—about motivation, preferences, rationality—that constrain our ability to understand and evaluate incentives themselves. The expansion of the term "incentives" to cover almost every sort of motivation and choice has exacerbated this problem. But without a vocabulary that allows us to distinguish among different kinds of motivations and preferences, we cannot distinguish ethical choices from unethical ones.

Incentives, Market Forces, and Institutional Constraints

The second way in which the meaning of "incentive" has changed is that the boundaries of the concept have expanded to include almost any feature of the environment that affects people's choices: we speak of "structural incentives" and "institutional incentives." Situational constraints are called "incentives," and so are market forces. All of these are quite different from an incentive understood as a bonus—an offer of an extrinsic benefit deliberately designed to alter a person's behavior in a particular way.

It is not surprising that the boundaries have been blurred. All of these conceptions can be subsumed under a very general notion of the factors that influence our choices or motivate action, and "incentives" has come to carry this general meaning.

Nonetheless, if our concern is the ethical use of incentives, it is important to recognize certain distinctions among these different types of motivating factors. Some are intentionally designed, while others are unintentional or automatic. Some are intrinsic reasons, while others are extrinsic factors. Some are factors operating in cooperative bargaining situations, while others are expressions of power relations. Ethical judgments require attending to these distinctions. For the purposes of this discussion, then, "incentives" will be used rather narrowly to mean an extrinsic benefit deliberately designed to alter behavior.

Recall that in the early twentieth century when the term was introduced, "incentive" had this narrow meaning. In psychology, incentives served as motivators in the absence of the automatic forces of instinct. In industry, incentives were used when market forces failed to motivate people in certain directions. The historical discussion revealed that "incentives" were originally understood in contradistinction to the automatic forces of the market and as a corrective for them. But today we often use "incentives" as a synonym for market forces.[9]

Consider the operations of an economic market. If one company lowers the price of its product, we might readily say that other companies now have an incentive to lower theirs. But we would not say that the first company *offered* all other companies an incentive to lower their prices. Buyers and sellers, thinking only of their own interests, make choices that affect the environment in which other buyers and sellers make their choices. But market forces are not conscious and intentional, and their rationale is intrinsic to the economic process itself. We might just as well say in this situation that the first company's lower price is a good reason for other companies to lower theirs, given that they need to remain competitive. The term "incentive" says nothing that "reason" cannot say just as well in this case, and we might well use the two terms interchangeably.

As another example, let us return to Sophocles' Philoctetes, the Greek warrior stranded on his island with a festering sore foot.[10] Neoptolemus tries to persuade him to leave the island

and join the Greeks besieging Troy. He tells Philoctetes that if he leaves his island and comes to Troy, he will be able to get medical care for his foot. This opportunity for healing would be an intrinsic consequence of Philoctetes' choice. We might well say today either that this is a good reason to return to Troy or that it is an incentive to return to Troy. But there is a distinction worth recognizing between "incentive" used in this sense and "incentive" used to describe, let us say, an offer from Neoptolemus of golden armor or three triremes if Philoctetes will agree to return to Troy. This Neoptolemus does not do. He does not go beyond persuasion to offer a bargain. He does not decide to introduce an extrinsic factor into the situation in order to induce Philoctetes to change his mind. The distinction between pointing out that medical care is available in Troy and offering some golden armor involves both the differences between the implicit, necessary consequences of an action and extrinsic factors and the differences between unintended features of the situation and those intentionally produced by a conscious agent.[11] In both of these respects, the differences between the two cases resemble the differences between market forces and incentives.

In the ideal market, we have only equal, individual rational actors whose choices are constrained by impersonal forces, which, like the force of gravity, operate equally upon us all. A trade will occur only if both parties act voluntarily for their own benefit. To the extent that incentives have become assimilated to our thinking about market forces, they appear to be implicitly ethical or, at least, benign. Controversial ethical and political issues are concealed, and incentives take on the positive ethical patina associated with the free market. By analogy, the voluntary, mutually beneficial, cooperative, and egalitarian characteristics inherent in ideal market transactions are assumed too readily and uncritically to characterize all other incentives as well.

Power relations are particularly likely to be overlooked when all incentives are assimilated to market transactions or systemic features of institutional systems. When incentives are in fact deliberate tools of policy, the equality of the parties involved ought not to be assumed. Often the party doing the offering has less to lose if his offer is rejected than the one doing the choosing has to lose by refusing the offer. The bargaining power of the parties depends on how badly each needs to reach an agreement.[12] One must ask: "Is the bargaining power of the parties equivalent?" "Is their relationship one of reciprocity?" "Can both parties simply walk away from a bad bargain?"

We may not think to ask these questions if we view incentives as automatic forces in the system or as inherent features of the institutional environment. We tend to speak of incentives in the passive voice—"What are the incentives in this situation?"— even when incentives are offered by someone to someone else with a clear and deliberate design. When the sense of "incentives" is broadly understood, and the distinction between deliberate and unintentional incentives is lost, the political character of relationships where incentives are employed deliberately—to alter what would otherwise be automatic outcomes—is entirely lost to view. In short, we need to remember that incentives are a form of power as well as a form of trade.[13]

There are many ways that those with power can structure institutions to affect people's choices. Offering a benefit or a bonus is just one of them. For example, different voting procedures produce different outcomes. So do different default options. The results will be different if a certain sum is automatically deducted from your paycheck to support charity unless you "opt out" than if you don't have to give unless you "opt in"—and different still if your employer doesn't support charitable payroll deductions and you have to sit down and write a check. Control of the available options is an effective tool also. For example, powerful countries could set up a trade regime such that less powerful countries will have to go along, since they no longer have the option of the old status quo.[14] Even something as simple as altering how the food is arranged in the school cafeteria can affect students' choices. These sorts of techniques are sometimes called "choice architecture," "agenda setting," or just plain "manipulation."[15] Does it make sense to include all of them in the umbrella category of "incentives"?

Yes and no. There are reasons why they tend to be lumped together, but the differences between them are as important as the similarities. "Choice architecture" changes the background conditions of one's choices, but, unlike an incentive, it does not increase the available options. Like incentives and unlike market exchanges, choice architecture deliberately attempts to shape people's choices, albeit without the transparency that incentives have. Institutional design also can be a powerful tool of social control without actually employing incentives at all. Consider Jeremy Bentham's architectural design, the Panopticon, meant to create institutions that would control people's actions through constant supervision. The rationale is based on the observation that preventing infractions depends on a combination of the severity of punishment and the likelihood of detection.[16] The thinking was that if detection could be increased to 100 percent through constant supervision and inspection, punishment would become virtually unnecessary. This is a logic that has nothing whatever to do with the logic of incentives as a means of motivating choices or of encouraging adaptive behavior.

In other words, there is a large set of ways in which situations can be structured to control behavior. Institutional design is one of them. Incentives are another member of this set. There is also another set of actions, consisting of types of bargains or exchanges. The idealized, cooperative market exchange where I trade my extra apples for your extra oranges is one of them. Incentives are another member of this set. Incentives stand at the intersection of the two sets—a form of trade that is also a form of power.

It is the ethical dimensions of incentives thus understood that interest me here. Of course, ethical issues can be raised about market forces: What is a fair price? Does the actual market approximate the ideal? Is the distribution of resources just? And ethical issues can be raised about agenda setting and choice architecture: Is the voting procedure fair? Is the cafeteria set up to promote healthy eating or maximum profits?[17] And in fact, similar ethical issues often arise in considering many different kinds of incentives—incentives in the broadest sense. Nonetheless, the differences in kind are important, and a narrower definition of incentives will help focus the ethical considerations.

Incentives "Strictly Speaking"

We are now in a position to specify a core understanding or a distinctive meaning of the concept of incentives—what we might call incentives "strictly speaking." Of course, I am not claiming that this is the only correct way to use the term, and neither do I expect to change the general linguistic practice. "Incentive" and "incentivize" will continue to be used very broadly, I am sure. But that broad usage blurs some very important distinctions. For all of the reasons discussed here and for the sake of clarity moving forward, we would benefit from putting some boundaries to the concept.

Incentives "strictly speaking" are a particular kind of offer:

1. an extrinsic benefit or a bonus that is neither the natural or automatic consequence of an action nor a deserved reward or compensation;

2. a discrete prompt expected to elicit a particular response; and

3. an offer intentionally designed to alter the status quo by motivating a person to choose differently than he or she would be likely to choose in its absence.

If the desired action would result naturally or automatically, no incentive would be necessary. An incentive is the added element without which the desired action probably would not occur. Thus, it is central to the core meaning of incentives that they are an instrument of government in the most general sense: they aim to direct people's behavior. (The emergence of the term historically within discourses of social control illustrates this point.) As such, an "incentive" offer often is made between people with unequal bargaining power. And such offers often are made in the context of an authority relationship—adult-child, employer-employee, government-citizen, government-organization, and so forth.

It is with this understanding that we turn now to look at the problem of the ethics of incentives in order to articulate standards for judgment. Incentives are one of the various ways in which people can get other people to do what they want them to do. They involve relations of power, power that is exercised in a manner distinguishable from persuasion as well as from coercion. The general problem, then, is how to distinguish legitimate from illegitimate uses of power altogether. The problem of distinguishing between legitimate and illegitimate uses of incentives is a subset of this.

The first step is to consider incentives in relation to coercion and persuasion so as to illuminate the ethical dimensions of their use. It is to this that I now turn.

Chapter FOUR

ETHICAL AND NOT SO ETHICAL INCENTIVES

How CAN ONE PERSON get another person to do what she wants him to do? The classic alternatives are force and persuasion: I can make you do what I want you to do or I can convince you to want to do what I want you to do. But I can also give you something that you want in exchange for your compliance with what I want. This is bargaining (of which incentives are a type), and it is one more form of power, along with coercion and persuasion. Each form of power is sometimes legitimate and sometimes not. Examining the standards for the legitimacy of all kinds of power will help clarify the criteria for distinguishing legitimate from illegitimate uses of incentives.

Coercion, Persuasion, and Bargaining

Generally speaking, the ethical superiority of persuasion to coercion is taken for granted. Moreover, this judgment of the relation between them has important political implications—it grounds claims for free and democratic government. Aristotle famously argues that the human capacity for *logos*, which can be translated as "speech" or "reason," is the condition for a self-governing political community.[1] The very first paper in the *Federalist Papers* poses the alternatives this way: "whether societies of men are really capable or not of establishing good government from *reflection and choice*, or whether they are forever destined to depend . . . on *accident and force*."[2] The superiority of persuasion to force is commonly tied in Western thought to the view that rationality is the distinctive human characteristic. Beasts, lacking reason, are not amenable to persuasion and can be subjected rightly to "brute force"—note the term.

Supposing that persuasion is ethically superior to coercion, how might incentives appear in relation to these other forms of power? The continuum might look something like this:

Coercion (force) ——— Bargaining (exchange) ——— Persuasion (speech)
←less desirable ————————————————————— more desirable→

Figure 1

We could proceed in this way, as if coercion lies at one end of the ethical spectrum and persuasion lies at the other, moving from least desirable to most desirable as we move from left to right. Now, we could ask ourselves, "Are incentives more like persuasion or more like coercion?" Or we might consider whether incentives are legitimate when the alternative to their use is force (e.g., the argument for economic sanctions in international relations) but illegitimate whenever persuasion is a viable option.

But, as is so often the case, upon reflection, the situation becomes considerably more complicated—and Figure 1 does *not* capture the complexities. There are varieties of coercion as well as varieties of persuasion, and they are not all equally legitimate. The use of force includes the legitimate police powers of the state as well as tyranny; it includes a fair fight as well as overpowering the defenseless. Persuasion, too, is not a simple category.

It includes rational deliberation but also begging, flattery, and fraud. It includes courtship as well as seduction, propaganda as well as the give-and-take of community meetings.[3]

Moreover, not every form of persuasion is ethically superior to every form of coercion or to every form of bargaining, for that matter. Incentives, for example, are usually clear and explicit attempts to influence someone's behavior, which might well be considered ethically superior to deceptive and hypocritical attempts at persuasion that mask their true intent.[4]

In the preface, we considered the opening scene of Sophocles' *Philoctetes*, where Neoptolemus, who would gladly fight to get what he wants, is reluctant to employ a deceitful scheme to achieve his ends. For him, deceit is a dishonorable way to overpower an opponent. Cicero concurs with this judgment, arguing that there are two ways of doing injustice: force and fraud. Both are beastly, but in his view, fraud is worse.[5] Perhaps we ought to question the claim that persuasion is categorically superior to coercion as an ethical mode of exercising power.

Moreover, the categories—coercion, bargaining, and persuasion—can be defined in different ways, and in almost every case, the definitions have powerful ethical and political implications. Consider, for example, how Machiavelli revised Cicero's view. According to Machiavelli, there are two ways of fighting: force and law. Force, the way of beasts, is divided into the way of the lion, using strength, and the way of the fox, using cunning. According to this analysis, deception *is* a kind of force.[6] Thomas Hobbes restricts the meaning of coercion so much that almost nothing counts as coercive, while Michel Foucault expands its meaning so greatly that almost everything appears to be coercive. For Hobbes, an absolute monarch is no more coercive than a republican sovereign, and so is at least equally legitimate. For Foucault, the bureaucratic "discipline" of modernity replaces the physical violence of the Middle Ages but serves the same purposes of control and coercion, and so is at least equally illegitimate.[7] Thus, neither of these approaches is helpful for sustaining meaningful ethical distinctions between legitimate and illegitimate exercises of power—but, for these authors, that is the point.

There is a similar variety of definitions when it comes to persuasion. Adam Smith, for example, characterizes bargaining as a form of persuasion and, as such, identifies it as a distinctively human capacity. Dogs can beg at the table, but they cannot bargain one bone for another.[8] In Smith's account, the relatively high ethical status of persuasion thus becomes attached to bargaining as well. Some contemporary economists and political scientists, on the other hand, argue to the contrary that there is no persuasion; what looks like persuasion is actually information exchange.[9] Thus, the possibility of any ethical critique of bargaining from the point of view of the superior claims of persuasion disappears, and bargaining can claim superiority to the only other alternative, coercion.[10] In short, the way in which the categories are defined shapes the ethical questions that arise and how they are addressed.

Both because of the complex variety of phenomena within each of the categories of power and because the definitions of the categories themselves are so consequential, the simple continuum of Figure 1 is misleading. The problem of definition is also humbling. No single set of definitions recommends itself above the others. How to proceed?

We are looking for a way of thinking about power that will be helpful in addressing the question at hand: how do we distinguish between legitimate and illegitimate uses of incentives? On what basis can such a judgment be made? As a form of power, incentives ought to be judged according to the same criteria as other forms of power. To discover those criteria requires maintaining the distinctions among categories of power rather than collapsing them—as well as employing definitions that do not already entail ethical judgments. With these considerations in mind, then, I offer the definitions that follow.

Power, in general, I take to be the capacity to achieve one's purposes—including, more specifically, the capacity to affect the actions of *others* in order to achieve one's purposes.[11] There are many sources of power: wealth, status, the authority that comes with office, and so on. But whatever its sources, power is exercised principally in three ways. "Coercion" means "the use or threat of force to influence people's behavior"; "bargaining" means "the use of an exchange or the promise of an exchange of gains or losses to influence people's behavior"; and "persuasion" means "the use of speech or other symbols to influence people's judgment or behavior, apart from coercion or bargaining."[12]

Each of these can be manifested in stronger or weaker forms. Power comes with varying degrees of pressure: it ranges from control, where one can get others to act "against their will"; to strong influence, where others are pressured, enticed, or convinced to act "against their better judgment"; to mild influence, where others are led to choose one particular alternative among a set of alternatives otherwise indifferent to them.[13] It is common to see a simple continuum here, with "control" at one pole and "influence" at the other, and then to identify this continuum of degrees of power with the continuum from "coercion" to "persuasion" pictured in Figure 1.[14] The result is that "coercion" becomes identified with the greatest degree of power, and the term comes to mean "control," perhaps because people assume that usually one can only get people to act "against their will" by threatening the use of force.[15]

But to make this identification is a mistake for several reasons. First, it implies that persuasion is always weaker than coercion. That is not always the case. For example, a threat of force that is not credible is a weak degree of power, while an attempt to persuade me that relies heavily on my guilt feelings can produce a good deal of pressure to comply. Second, thinking in terms of the two overlapping continuums implies also that bargaining, located between coercion and persuasion, lies somewhere between control and influence as well. Yet bargaining does not fall at a single middle point between the two. For example, in the form of ideal market transactions, bargaining resembles rational persuasion in the minimal degree of pressure either party exerts on the other. In the form of blackmail, bargaining can exert a great deal of pressure indeed. Thus, the *degrees* of power must be distinguished from the *forms* of power if we want to account for the complexity of power—and thereby, incentives.

Standards of Legitimacy

We have noted that persuasion is usually considered ethically superior to force. But we have also noted that each category contains subcategories that could be ranked hierarchically from most to least legitimate (see Figure 2). Coercion includes law,[16] a fair fight, tyranny, conquest, and the threat of these. Incentives belong in the second category, bargaining, which includes many kinds of trades: market transactions, bribery, blackmail, and so forth.[17] Persuasion includes rational deliberation, begging, flattery, and fraud. These lists are meant to be suggestive, not exhaustive, and the order of the lists in the columns is not meant to be precise. But within each category, generally speaking, we would tend to judge the subcategories listed first more favorably than those listed later. Why? What are the implicit standards employed in making these judgments?

Coercion – Force	Bargaining – Exchange	Persuasion – Speech
Just Law – Authority	Trade	Rational Deliberation
Fair Fight	Exploitation	Flattery
Bullying	Undue Influence	Begging
Conquest	Bribery	Seduction
Tyranny	Blackmail	Fraud
Etc.	Etc.	Intimidation
		Etc.

Figure 2

I will argue that any one of these exercises of power can be judged according to three primary criteria:

first, by whether it serves a legitimate purpose;

second, by whether it allows a voluntary response; and

third, by its effect on the character of the parties involved.

For example, bribery invites a person to violate his duty; its purpose is illegitimate and it undermines character as well. One of the reasons that tyranny is illegitimate is that it violates the principle of consent or voluntariness. Another reason is that it turns political power from its proper purposes. Concerns with character are raised by some forms of bargaining—for example, incentive systems that encourage people to ask only "what's in it for me?"—and by some forms of persuasion—for example, demagogic political rhetoric that motivates people by appealing to their worst passions.

These criteria explain why a fair fight might be considered morally superior to fraud or deception. In a case of fraud, the dupe is really not in a position to choose freely, since informed consent is not possible, and the second criterion is violated. In a fair fight (understood as one in which both parties have an equal chance to emerge victorious) the combatants are fully informed, able to influence the outcome by their own actions, and voluntarily join in combat. To take an example from the realm of love: all three criteria are evidently at work in the distinction between courtship and seduction, two quite different forms of persuasion. Courtship is a relationship of mutuality aimed at establishing a loving commitment. Its purpose is legitimate; its aspect is consensual; and it can bring out the best in people. A seduction aims at the selfish gratification of one person with no regard for the well-being of the other; it is often conducted under false pretenses and exploits the weakness of one party so that the mutuality of freely given consent is put in question;[18] and it proceeds by encouraging moral weakness.

While the first two criteria seem fairly obvious—that is, the legitimacy of the aim and the voluntariness of the action—the concern with character requires some explanation.[19] On one level, character means nothing more than the tendency or predisposition to behave in certain ways—a person's characteristic way of doing things. But when we say that a person *has* character, we typically mean that he or she has a strong or a good character, that is, that this person is unlikely to be swayed from behaving according to his or her characteristic dispositions and that those dispositions are good. Power is relevant to character. The various ways in which power is exercised in a given social setting, and the sorts of things that are used to influence people's decisions, have an impact both on people's characteristic dispositions and on what good character is understood to be.

The matter of character goes beyond consideration of individuals to include concerns with institutional culture as well. Institutional culture could be seen as character "writ large." What are the ways "we" characteristically behave in this organization? Are we encouraged to feel, and expected to feel, loyalty to the organization and to "go the extra mile" for the group when necessary? Is there a team spirit or an expectation that everyone should look out for himself or herself? The way that power is exercised within an institution will have a great deal to do with how questions such as these are answered.

People can be led and governed in a variety of ways that make a difference for good character. Power relationships can have an impact on the character of all of the individuals involved in any particular interaction: both those who are engaged in making an offer, persuading, or threatening force and those who are responding to offers, arguments, or threats. For example, to offer a bribe is corrupt—but to accept it is also corrupting to the extent that it weakens the disposition to put duty above interest. Some people respond to flattery more readily than others. Flattering them certainly encourages their vanity. And those who habitually get their way through flattery are affected by it as well. Flatterers are hypocritical. Children who are bullied by adults often become bullies themselves. The ways in which bargaining, persuasion, and coercion are employed can have profound effects on character.

Not only what we do but why we do it have a bearing on moral character. A person who sometimes does the wrong thing for the right reason is more trustworthy than a person who sometimes does the right thing for the wrong reason. It makes an ethical difference, both for individual character and for social norms, whether people are motivated by fear of punishment, desire for gain, generosity, rectitude, and so forth.[20] Coercion, bargaining, and persuasion are all tied to different motivations. And so effect on character must be one of the criteria for assessing the forms of power.

These three considerations, then—whether the purpose of a power transaction is legitimate; whether the choice made by the subject is voluntary; and the way the transaction impacts character—ground the lists in Figure 2. Moreover, it is easy to see that for each form of power there is an ideal type where all of the criteria are met. If there is also a rough equality among the parties to a power transaction, you might argue that the ideal case becomes a relationship of cooperation: nobody is in a position to impose his or her will; all parties retain their autonomy. For example, we could describe the ideal case of coercion to be the exercise of law where the laws derive their authority from the voluntary consent of the people and are limited to legitimate purposes, like security and prosperity. The rule of law is a form of social cooperation meant to preclude the imposition of arbitrary, private will. Similarly, the ideal form of bargaining is one among equal parties acting both autonomously and cooperatively: something as simple as my selling you my old car.

Finally, consider persuasion in the form of rational deliberation. If there is a convincing logic to support the choice of a course of action, part of that logic will be a justification of its purpose. To act on the basis of your own conviction is to be guided by reason, to be self-governing, and hence to act voluntarily—the choice is unconstrained, not only by external forces but also by internal influences of passion and desire. Many might also say that self-government in this sense is also a sign of good character. Self-government is virtue to the extent that it involves subjecting the passions to the government of the higher faculties of reason. The person who is self-governing in this respect is, thus, also a person of good moral character, tending to act reasonably and unlikely to be moved from his or her rational convictions.

Thus the ideal form of persuasion, like the ideal forms of coercion and bargaining, respects human freedom and rationality. In effect, the three criteria I have suggested amount to the claim that any act of power ought to be judged by whether or not it respects the character of human beings as free and rational.

I began by asking "what are the implicit standards employed" when making judgments about power. But of course we cannot simply rely on commonsense intuitions to supply a foundation for ethical argument. Intuitions need to be subjected to examination and their premises exposed. In this case, the examination revealed the premise that human beings ought to respected as free and rational; that is to say, they ought to be treated in a way that respects their dignity. This premise is the basis for our shared intuitions about the legitimacy and illegitimacy of power in its various modes. Indeed, this premise could be seen as the minimal grounding for ethical inquiry itself. It would make little sense to undertake a project to establish criteria for ethical judgment if one did not presuppose that people are capable of making judgments and guiding their conduct by them. Thus, when I assert that people ought to be treated with dignity, which is to say, respected as free and rational, what I mean by that is that they ought to be treated as independent agents capable of moral responsibility.[21]

But what do we mean by "freedom" and "rationality"? Obviously these concepts are susceptible to widely varying interpretations: there is enormous disagreement as to what counts as "freedom" and what counts as "rationality." For Thomas Hobbes, for example, even the agreement to submit to a conquering army counts as legitimate consent and an act of freedom.[22] For Immanuel Kant, on the other hand, free action can only proceed on a pure rational principle. For this reason, the response to an incentive can lead to morally commendable actions, but those actions will not have the "authentic moral worth" of actions done exclusively from duty.[23] The opposition between Kant and Hobbes echoes that between the "moralists" and the "Mandevillians" mentioned earlier. In short, we might secure agreement on the specific criteria for legitimacy—legitimacy of purpose, voluntariness, and character—and we might even secure agreement on their deeper ground, namely that legitimate incentives must respect human freedom and rationality, but, without greater specification of the key concepts, we will not have provided workable standards.

In contemporary economic theory, rationality and freedom are minimally construed. Rationality does not refer to the capacity to regulate the passions or to judge among human purposes. It only requires adjusting beliefs to the available evidence and acting consistently with your preferences given the constraints and opportunities in your situation. Reasoning is understood to be a form of calculating for the sake of maximizing utility.[24] Freedom is also minimally defined. The requirements of freedom are met by voluntariness, that is, having alternatives and the capacity to choose among them.

But freedom construed minimally as voluntariness is problematic, particularly if (as Hobbes would have it) a choice "counts" as voluntary even when it is made under threat of coercion.[25] Isaiah Berlin made the point with respect to the insufficiency of voluntariness thus understood when he wrote: "If in a totalitarian state I betray my friend under threat of torture . . . I can reasonably say that I did not act freely. Nevertheless, I did, of course, make a choice . . . the mere existence of alternatives is not, therefore, enough to make my action free (although it may be voluntary) in the normal sense of the word."[26] To judge this sort of torture as an unethical abuse of power requires a conception of freedom that means something more than merely making a choice.

The minimalist conception of rationality employed in contemporary economic theory also makes it difficult to judge the ethics of incentives. According to that theory, all choices are made essentially for the same reason: to maximize utility. People act rationally when they choose the course of action that gives them the most of what they prefer. An incentive adds a benefit to the balance of costs and benefits that determines a person's choice. To calculate that balance and to act accordingly is to act rationally. Contrast this with the notion of reason implied in an attempt to rationally persuade someone to make a certain choice. Such persuasion implies that you can understand and assess the options "on the merits." Depending on the circumstances, some arguments will count as good reasons for choosing "a" instead of choosing "b" and others won't.

To illustrate: where incentives are employed instead of persuasion, it can be an insult to be offered an incentive—and in three different ways. First, it might imply that you are crass, that is, that there is no good reason for you to do the thing you are being asked to do but that your compliance can be bought. Second, it might imply that you are stupid and would not be able to appreciate the good reasons for doing what you are being asked to do so that an appeal to your selfish interests must take the place of argument. Third, it might imply that you are not well-intentioned and must be induced to do the right thing by extrinsic benefits, since you would not respond positively to the good reasons to do it.[27]

For example, teachers might well be insulted when they are offered a bonus to adopt a certain method of teaching reading in the classroom. As professionals, they might expect to be treated with respect for their expertise and for their ability to compare the intrinsic qualities of the competing reading programs and to decide accordingly—rational decision in quite a different sense than utility calculation. They might also be insulted by being offered a bonus if the scores of their minority students improve relative to those of their white students. Incentive systems in this case carry the implication that the problem of the minority achievement gap is a problem of neglect on the part of the teachers. If they cannot be motivated to serve minority students for the right reasons, perhaps they can be motivated by the promise of a reward.*

But if we stick with the minimalist understanding of rationality, it makes no difference whether teachers are persuaded or "incentivized" to adopt a certain course of action. In either case, they act "rationally" by making the choice that conforms most closely to their preferences. "Good reasons" cannot be distinguished from any other kind of reasons, and the matter of professional respect goes unrecognized. Consequently, the use of incentives in cases like these appears to be perfectly legitimate, and the feeling of insult that accompanies the incentive is simply inexplicable. That feeling of insult only makes sense when a broader understanding of rationality is in play, one that includes consideration of a course of action "on the merits."

When freedom and rationality are defined more expansively, incentives will be subjected to stricter scrutiny. We might move, for example, from mere voluntariness and calculation as governing conceptions toward autonomy—where human freedom would be understood to include the capacity to set one's own ends or purposes according to a rational standard. Making this move increases the likelihood that incentives will be judged illegitimate when they are paternalistic, manipulative, or exploitative. These "gray areas" between total control and benign influence can all be considered assaults on autonomy. Paternalism can be described as treating another person as if he is incapable of recognizing for himself what his purposes ought to be or of rationally pursuing them; manipulation as a broad category of actions that deceive a person into believing that he is acting

---

*Of course, teacher neglect may be contributing to the problem, and incentives may motivate teachers to increase their efforts either for the sake of the benefit or because the incentive signals the importance of addressing the problem. The fact that incentives can be insulting may not be sufficient reason to rule out their use.

autonomously when he is actually being used for someone else's purposes; and exploitation as taking advantage of another's weakness to secure his compliance in subordinating his own ends to yours. (Note that seduction might be considered a particular kind of exploitation where the weaker party is also deceived as to the true purposes of the stronger.)[28]

Incentives, as a form of power, are sometimes deployed in all of these ways. To distinguish their proper use from abusive uses requires applying the standard that human beings ought to be treated as free and rational. Where freedom and rationality are understood in a robust sense, as the components of autonomous moral agency, paternalism, manipulation, and exploitation are more likely to be considered illegitimate.[29]

Where, then, does this leave us? On the most abstract level, any particular instance of the use of an incentive or disincentive can be understood as an exercise of power. Power is legitimate only to the extent that the parties involved are treated with human dignity, which is to say, treated as beings capable of moral agency on account of their rationality and capacity for freedom. People should not be governed as if they were beasts, through the exercise of brute force.

Somewhat more concretely, this means that acts of power can be judged by whether they serve a rationally defensible purpose, whether they allow for a voluntary response or are based on freely given consent, and whether they accord with the requirements of moral character. These are the conceptual materials we can use to distinguish between legitimate and illegitimate incentives, just as we would distinguish between the use and abuse of other forms of power. We are not condemned to choose between the posture of the "moralists," who find all incentives reprehensible, and that of the "Mandevillians," who embrace them.

What remains to be considered is whether the standards for legitimacy identified here are helpful in sorting through the ambiguities and competing claims involved when incentives are proposed as solutions to practical policy problems. Are the concepts employed—legitimacy of purpose, voluntariness, and character—adequate to encompass the ethics of actual power relationships? Since we do not live in an ideal world, how do we judge among imperfect alternatives?

Indeed, the application of standards turns out to be a complex affair. As with all prudential judgments, context matters greatly. There is no "rule of thumb" that allows for a mechanical application of the standards. Nonetheless, they can provide significant guidance for judgment, as we will see.

Chapter FIVE

Applying Standards, Making Judgments

How can we determine whether any particular use of incentives is ethical? I have been arguing that these judgments can be made best when incentives are understood as a form of power and evaluated accordingly. The ethical issues are more readily apparent when incentives are understood in this way, and standards of legitimacy can be clearly identified that apply to all forms of power: legitimacy of purpose, voluntariness, and effect on character.

Articulating these criteria allows us to identify what sorts of questions need to be asked in judging incentives. The federal government, aiming to decrease traffic deaths, gives highway funds only to states that raise the drinking age: is that a legitimate objective of federal authority? The International Monetary Fund (IMF) offers loans to governments on the condition that they adopt certain policies. The governments most in need of such loans are those that cannot tap private financial markets. Is the cost of refusing the loans "prohibitive," effectively leaving the governments without a choice? To help teach a sense of social responsibility, students are sometimes given incentives to volunteer for community service. Does this practice build the altruistic qualities of character that are sought? Or does offering the incentive actually reinforce self-interestedness? Is there a positive or a negative effect on character? These sorts of questions are the starting point for ethical analysis of incentives, and examples could be multiplied.

Since a primary purpose of the discussion thus far has been to bring ethical difficulties to the fore, I may have given the impression that I am deeply suspicious of incentives. Suspicion, however, is not the same as blanket condemnation: the idea is to identify criteria for discriminating among incentives. It is worth emphasizing that the perspective I have been advocating allows for the legitimacy of many, perhaps even most, incentives. Many uses of incentives are straightforward: express traffic lanes for cars carrying more than two passengers during rush hour, offers of low-cost insurance to members of voluntary civic organizations[1]—these are clear cases.[2] They meet the three criteria of legitimacy of purpose, voluntariness, and benign impact on character without raising any additional difficulties.

Nonetheless, in many cases, additional difficulties cannot be avoided. Having established the three criteria and knowing what questions to ask, our problems are often just beginning. Each of the three criteria is ambiguous and contestable in various ways. What if there are multiple competing purposes? What counts as "voluntary"? How much should considerations of character matter? Our questions multiply. And finally, satisfying all three conditions is always necessary, but only sometimes sufficient, to reach a judgment that an incentive is legitimate.

Additional factors arise from the complexities of particular situations. Thus far, we have considered the relation between the agent offering the incentive and the person or organization responding to the offer without considering the broader context in which they operate. Taking context into account, we note first that an incentive might be perfectly legitimate when offered by one person but not so when offered by another with a different status. A university administration might offer incentives to support a certain line of biomedical research. Different questions arise when the same offer is made by a pharmaceutical company. Second, a legitimate offer made to some people but not to others similarly situated is unfair. A company offering bonuses to encourage early retirement should make that offer to everyone within the same category of age or service to the company. And finally, in assessing incentives in a given setting, we need to know whether they work and how well they work compared to the alternatives. These sorts of questions—about undue influence, equity, and effectiveness—can be added to the list of questions about purpose, voluntariness, and character.

These are just some of the reasons why there is no "rule of thumb" that can be mechanically applied to determine the legitimacy or illegitimacy of incentives in every case. These sorts of determinations always require an exercise of judgment. The discussion that follows explores some of the complexities that arise when considering incentives in practice in a wide variety of policy areas in order to show how judgments concerning the use of incentives might be made well.

Purpose, Voluntariness, Character

Consider a case that illustrates the problem of multiple, competing purposes. Cost containment in health care is a legitimate purpose. It even could be argued that medical professionals have an ethical responsibility to do something about rising medical costs. In addition, insurance companies that pay out medical benefits have a private, financial interest in cost containment. As an incentive for doctors to contain costs, some health maintenance organizations (HMOs) instituted "capitation plans"— giving doctors a flat sum per patient and allowing the doctors to keep any remaining funds if they spend less than the allotment.[3]

These plans can serve the legitimate purpose of cost containment in health care. There are no problematic issues concerning voluntariness or character, and the incentive system appears to be beyond reproach.

But it is not sufficient to establish that an incentive serves *a* legitimate purpose. In this situation, there are conflicting purposes, both legitimate. Cost containment is important, but the doctor also must deliver the best care he or she can to patients. To the extent that a capitation plan creates incentives for the doctor to undertreat patients, it is a clear case of bribery and cannot be considered legitimate. The doctor receives money for neglecting his or her primary duty and serving the interests of the one offering the money instead—in this case, the insurance company. Indeed, this very problem was the heart of a U.S. Supreme Court case brought in 2000. The plaintiff claimed that provision of medical services under terms rewarding physicians for limiting medical care violated the insurance company's responsibility "since the terms created an incentive to make decisions in the physicians' self-interest, rather than the plan participants' exclusive interests."[4]

If incentives could be structured so that they only go so far as to discourage overtreatment of patients (e.g., to diminish the number of unnecessary caesarean sections), then there would be no conflict of purposes between optimum health care and cost containment, and the incentives would be legitimate.[5]

A similar analysis might be applied to incentives given to police officers to issue a certain number of traffic tickets per day. Traffic fees are a legitimate source of revenue for city governments. And there is no problem when traffic tickets are issued only to those who violate traffic laws. But prioritizing the raising of revenue by instituting ticket quotas can produce injustices; police officers are induced to behave in a way that is equivalent to the doctor who "undertreats" patients. An incentive that serves a legitimate purpose must be judged ethically illegitimate when it undermines a more important competing purpose.

Turning to the criterion of voluntariness, we are confronted with a different sort of difficulty. We have already seen that determining what counts as "voluntary" can be a vexed question. In considering the ethics of incentives, concerns have focused on what are called "irresistible offers" or "coercive offers"—offers where a person doesn't "really" have a choice. Can an offer be so attractive, so difficult for a vulnerable person to resist, that it is tantamount to coercion? Is it coercive to offer a large sum of money to a homeless person to participate in a risky drug trial? Can the offer of a reduced sentence in exchange for a guilty plea coerce an innocent person into pleading guilty because the risks of a harsher sentence make pleading innocent no longer a "real" option? In that case, isn't the prosecutor like the gunman who offers a choice between "your money or your life"?[6] Or consider the case of a "lecherous millionaire" who offers to pay for a child's expensive and life-saving surgery if the child's mother will become his mistress.[7] Is this a freedom-enhancing offer or a coercive act?

Offers seem suspect where the cost of refusing the offer is "prohibitive." This is the possibility raised by the example of the IMF at the beginning of the chapter. Similarly, the cost to the mother of refusing the "lecherous millionaire's" offer is the lost opportunity to save her child's life. Sometimes an offer can exert sufficient pressure to get people to act "against their better judgment," to make choices about which they have principled objections or serious misgivings. Is a person free to choose in a meaningful sense if he or she has no acceptable alternative?[8]

Alan Wertheimer and Franklin Miller argue that the absence of an acceptable alternative is only one of two conditions of coerced consent. The other is the presence of a threat to deprive a person of a right. "Your money or your life" is the classic example of coercion. To give up your money under these circumstances is not a voluntary act. If this is correct, an actual offer cannot be coercive, since there is no threatened deprivation of a right.[9] The person who accepts an offer, even an odious one, acts voluntarily and gives consent. After all, the "lecherous million-aire" could not be prosecuted for rape if the woman accepted his offer.*

But just because offers or incentives cannot be coercive, there is no reason to conclude that they cannot be unethical. We *should* be concerned about the behavior of the "lecherous mil-lionaire" but not because the magnitude of his largesse made his offer "irresistible" and hence coercive. There is nothing wrong with offering large sums of money to poor people. Had he asked the woman to do his gardening, there would not be the same problem here. Offering large incentives to homeless people for research participation for innocuous research, like filling out a questionnaire, might be foolish, but nobody would think of it as coercive or unethical. The ethical question arises only because people are being asked to do something they are reluctant to do for some reason. Otherwise, there would be no need for a large incentive. One relevant factor in assessing the incentive, then, is what that reason might be.

The hypothetical example presupposes that the woman finds the prospect of becoming the millionaire's mistress unappealing, to say the least. And, in this case, that feeling ought to be re-spected. Brian Barry asks on what grounds we might rightly dis-approve of deals that people nonetheless have a right to make. And his response includes offers that are corrupting and offers that exploit a person's economic weakness, particularly if they express contempt or are degrading.[10] The millionaire's behavior fits this description, and he can be criticized for the terms that he offers. Offers such as these are seductive or exploitative and an inappropriate use of influence—they are often called "undue influence" or "undue inducement"—and, while they do not con-stitute coercion, they are unethical nonetheless.

---

*In Shakespeare's *Measure for Measure*, Isabel refuses a similar offer, al-though she could save her brother's life by complying, saying that it is better that her brother die once than that her soul suffer eternally.

A careful consideration of the question of voluntariness leads to additional questions.[11] We need to ask not only "Is this voluntary?" but also "Is this incentive seductive or exploitative?" Is it an "undue inducement"?

Finally, in applying the standards, difficulties can arise over which of the three standards ought to matter most. Sometimes an incentive system designed to effectively fulfill an important purpose may compromise voluntariness or have potential negative effects on character. A judgment must be made as to which of the standards should have priority. In my view, judgments about balancing the criteria should take account of the context. In the military, for example, voluntariness has a different status than in civilian life because of the need for military discipline. Similarly, it makes sense to give less weight to the matter of character in the workplace than in the elementary school classroom, where character formation is part of the objective of the enterprise.

"Moralists," of course, tend to weigh considerations of character more heavily than others do. They are right to draw attention to the matter, at least. The character question often gets short shrift. But it is always a factor worth considering because incentives are fundamentally about motivation. Incentives are extrinsic motivators, and sometimes it is important that things be done for their intrinsic value. This is why incentives for "volunteer" community service are problematic. Paying students to get good grades raises a similar issue. One must ask, "Is incentive motivation appropriate in this domain?" There are some spheres of life (though by no means all) where it matters a great deal that things be done for the right reason.

Applying the standards, then, requires judgments of various kinds beyond the initial determination that the three basic criteria have been met, which is difficult enough. One must also consider matters like balancing competing legitimate purposes and judging among the standards when they come into conflict with one another.

Effectiveness, Equity, Undue Influence

The three criteria were initially identified by considering how one person might go about influencing another's behavior. We began with the question: "How can one person legitimately get another to do what she wants him to do?" But incentives are generally employed within systems and institutions where relationships are complex. The three basic criteria for legitimacy turn out to be minimal, threshold standards—necessary, but not always sufficient. There are additional questions to consider. I highlight here questions of effectiveness, equity, and undue influence in its classic form, "strings attached."

The first question, then, is: "Does this incentive system work better than the alternatives?" And this *is* an ethical question: in public policy, efficient use of resources is often an ethical responsibility. To the extent that we have a responsibility to protect the environment, effectiveness certainly ought to be one of the criteria employed in assessing market-based incentives for pollution control. Because medical research is crucial for public health, protocols that hinder research by making it difficult to recruit subjects carry an ethical burden. Incentives for recruiting research subjects may not be beyond reproach, but if they were effective as compared to persuasion alone, that would be one element in their favor. Economic sanctions in international affairs are a slightly different kind of case, but here, too, any defense of their use would have to include a showing that the sanctions are more likely to produce the desired result than any other course of action. It is not only useless, but also unethical, to expend public resources and cause hardships needlessly. When the question is whether to employ incentives, rather than coercion or persuasion, to meet a particular goal, the justification of the choice of incentives must include an assessment of their effectiveness in meeting that goal relative to the alternatives.

Would coercion work better? There is one respect in which coercion generally has an advantage over incentives: it provides the transparency necessary for accountability. Let us return to the example of incentives offered to physicians by HMOs. We said that the problem of conflicting purposes could be solved by structuring incentives so as to get the treatment decisions "just right" as far as is practically possible—neither overtreatment nor undertreatment. But a further problem arises if HMOs attempt to guide specific medical decisions through the structuring of incentives. Formally, the incentives present the doctors with a choice, and thus the criterion of voluntariness is met. This is why it is typically the physicians, and not the HMOs, who are held responsible for the results of medical treatment decisions.

But are the insurance companies truly without responsibility, when their policies are *designed* to steer treatment decisions in certain directions? In the U.S. Supreme Court case mentioned earlier, the petitioner claimed that even though a physician was the immediate medical provider, the doctor's responsibility was not final: the HMO had violated its fiduciary responsibility by encouraging treatment decisions harmful to the petitioner.

The example raises the general point that the use of incentive systems can mask responsibility. A straightforward regulation often makes accountability clearer and is one reason why coercion in the form of regulations is sometimes preferable to incentives. Knowing whom to blame is crucial for accountability. And when decision-makers know that they will be held accountable, they are more likely to be concerned about getting the job done well.

Would persuasion work better than incentives? There is one respect in which persuasion has a general advantage. Consider the effects of incentives on institutional culture. What happens to loyalty and responsibility within an organization once it becomes common to receive a bonus of some kind for each particular service to the institution? Programs that create the expectation of additional individual reward can undermine both fellowship and professionalism in organizations as different as sports teams, hospitals, and corporations. For example, consider a soccer team that pays each player for the goals he scores and thus discourages passes to other players who are better placed to score. Incentives can create a situation where people come to construe their responsibilities to the organization and its common enterprise narrowly. And once an institutional culture is transformed from one in which a team spirit is cultivated to one in which the prevailing norm is "each man for himself," individuals entering those organizations are affected accordingly—they are likely to be less altruistic where altruism is not expected or appreciated.

In other words, incentive programs instituted precisely to motivate employees can backfire in the long run.[12] Once the incentive stops, so does the motivation. If, on the other hand, people are encouraged to have a more expansive sense of their responsibilities to the enterprise, the effect is likely to be longer lasting. Recall that the definition of persuasion that I gave in chapter 4 is the only definition of a form of power that includes an impact on beliefs as well as behavior. Unless the behavior prompted by incentives can be transformed into habitual behavior and become part of accepted expectations, the impact of incentives could be short-lived and even corrosive. The long-term impact on institutional culture should be one of the considerations in answering the question, "Does it work?"

The next question is, "Is it fair?" This question drives the heated political and legal controversies over incentives offered by state and local governments to businesses to entice them to relocate. Many issues are involved in these controversies. First, some complain that incentives offered to a large company to relocate are a form of "corporate welfare," which uses taxpayers' money without bringing any benefits to the taxpayers. (Whether the incentives do or do not provide public benefits is an empirical question—and this is really the question of effectiveness in a different guise.)[13] Second, established local businesses, who did not receive any tax incentives in the past, argue that the government is providing an unfair advantage to their competitors. Third, some argue that the incentives are unfair to other states because they interfere with fair market competition among the states for business.[14] Whenever incentives benefit one or a few members of a group where the rest are similarly situated, the question of fairness or equity will arise.

And the fairness of incentives is an inherently problematic issue, as we saw in chapter 3, where incentives were distinguished from rewards and compensation. Do AIG executives deserve their retention bonuses? Most would say, of course not. But these bonuses are not put in place to reward hard work or high performance. They are incentives, not rewards, designed for the sole purpose of encouraging executives to choose to remain with the company. As I argued earlier, the right amount for an incentive is the amount it takes to get people to choose what the one offering the incentive wants them to choose. This is why we talk about "fair wages" or "just compensation" but not about "fair incentives."

Nonetheless, the fairness question is bound to arise. These bonuses are being paid out of taxpayers' money—for most people, out of wages that were earned with hard work and productive effort. And our general assumption is that money received from an employer ought to be earned. It is not surprising that thinking of executive bonuses as incentives does not make them more palatable to most people.

Last, but certainly not least, comes the question, "Are there 'strings attached'?" Incentives, particularly monetary incentives, come with conditions. You will receive a certain benefit if you do x, y, or z. The question is whether there are some conditions that are inappropriate, given the relationship between the parties. Take the case of the parents who stipulated in their will that their daughter would receive her inheritance only if she were a stay-at-home mom. Of course, the parents are free to make such stipulations in their will. And there would be nothing wrong with expressing their opinions and trying to persuade their daughter to be a stay-at-home mom. Yet, this is a case where the parents are trying to use the power of their money to influence an important life decision that is not theirs to make.

This, too, is a form of "undue influence." People or institutional agents are said to exercise undue influence when they exert power that they rightly wield in one area in an area in which they ought not to have any particular power, for example, when a person with money or fame influences political outcomes, jumps a queue, or receives special privileges to the detriment of others. In this case, we might say that the person is unduly influential; he or she gets something undeserved at others' expense. "Strings" attached to incentives use power in one sphere to influence outcomes in another, where the agent has no legitimate authority. And this is one kind of injustice.[15]

This type of undue influence should be distinguished from the undue influence or undue inducement that came up in the discussion of "coercive offers." In that case, a person exerts power on someone in a vulnerable position in a way that is inappropriate. Pressures of various sorts fall into this category, for example, where the cost of refusing an offer is "prohibitive" for the offeree and when the offer is corrupting. The term "undue influence" is used to refer both to these sorts of pressures and to transgressing the boundaries of one's authority.

How should we determine whether the conditions attached to incentives are legitimate or constitute undue influence in this second sense? There are strings attached to IMF and World Bank grants and loans to countries around the world.[16] In evaluating these incentives, considerations of character hardly come into play; the country is free to refuse the offer; and, if the purposes are legitimate, the incentive program would seem to meet all three criteria. But an ethical question remains. Loan conditions might include requirements for privatizing state enterprises, or limiting expansion of military spending, or imposing environmental regulations, or any number of things. All of these purposes might be perfectly laudable and legitimate ones, but they might not be within the legitimate purview of the authority of the IMF or World Bank.

Distinctions must be made between conditions directly related to the loan and the ability of the country to repay it and conditions that project the power of international institutions into areas where they do not belong. These are not always easy lines to draw, but, without the attempt to do so, there is no limit to the power of the global rich to dictate terms. It certainly could be argued that agents outside the country should not be able to pursue their own agendas for domestic political and social reform. And if the country receiving the loan is a democratic one, incentives with inappropriate conditions undermine democracy as well.

Similar issues arise in the relationship between the federal and state governments in the United States. By attaching conditions to federal grants, the federal government is able to influence state policies in areas where the states are the primary constitutional authorities. The No Child Left Behind Act, for example, involves many requirements that govern aspects of education that the federal government probably could not regulate directly. Of course, the states can refuse the money if they do not wish to comply with the program's requirements. But the cost of rejecting the offer of federal funds is often "prohibitive"—and so the two senses of "undue influence" come together. An agent can affect outcomes in an area where it has no authority by attaching "strings" to a very seductive offer. As in the case of the IMF, there are questions to be asked and lines to be drawn here as well.

Lest you mistakenly conclude that "strings attached" is only an issue between governments, let me offer one more example: course development grants. Money is offered to professors as a bonus if they agree to teach certain courses that would enhance the university's offerings in a certain area.[17] It is unlikely that this sort of program would cause any difficulties with regard to the legitimacy of its purpose or the freedom of the professor to choose to participate. Considerations of character hardly come into play. The incentive program meets all three primary criteria. Nonetheless, we are not finished. We need to ask who is offering the grant—the university, a private foundation, a private individual, or a commercial enterprise?

It certainly could be argued that where there are regular procedures for determining the university's curriculum, agents outside the university ought not to be able to pursue their own agendas in this way. There are systemic effects of such donations, effects on the university as a whole. At what point does the university as a corporate body of professional educators begin to lose control of its educational objectives? In this context, incentives can become a substitute for established processes of deliberation (persuasion) in making curriculum decisions.

Unrestricted giving or a gift to fund a program initiated by the university does not raise the same sorts of issues raised by grants for particular educational and research objectives set by the donor. There is also an issue here of character with respect to the donors, as well as an issue of the social norms governing elite behavior. In a democracy, it is particularly important for elites to appreciate the problems associated with the connection of wealth and influence. It is one thing to use your wealth to support an institution and another thing to use it to influence its agenda.[18]

Do I expect wealthy philanthropists to become more humble? Do I expect the World Bank, the IMF, and the U.S. government to exercise self-restraint? Not really. But I do want to revitalize some questions about our accepted practices. We have become so accustomed to "strings attached" in some of these areas that we don't even bat an eye. And one of the reasons that we don't is that nobody is forcing anyone to do anything. Incentives give people choices. Everything is voluntary. How can that be bad? I hope that this discussion has revealed the inadequacy of that simple logic.

To summarize: when incentives are considered as a form of power and compared to its other forms, multiple ethical questions rise to the surface. We need to ask, first:

- Does the incentive serve a legitimate purpose?
- Does it allow for a voluntary response?
- Does it affect character positively or not at all?

But it turns out that this is not enough. We also need to ask a number of other questions:

- Which of several purposes is most important here?
- Is the incentive seductive or exploitative?
- What is most important in this case: purpose, voluntariness, or character?
- Does the incentive work?
- Does it mask accountability?
- What will be its long-term impact on institutional culture?
- Is it fair?
- Is this incentive a legitimate use of power and not a case of "undue influence"?

In short, we need to consider all of the factors that arise in making judgments about the use and abuse of power, whatever its form.

Chapter SIX

Getting Down to Cases

Generally speaking, I have argued that incentives have not been controversial enough. But there are some areas where the question of the ethics of incentives has been controversial indeed. I take up four such controversies in this chapter to illustrate the sort of analysis that is required to distinguish legitimate from illegitimate incentives: plea bargaining, payment to recruit human subjects for medical research, conditions attached to loans by the International Monetary Fund, and incentives used to motivate children to learn.

These cases have some features in common, but I have deliberately chosen them from very different domains. Different areas of life have their own distinctive norms, which define the relationships of the actors and impact ethical judgments about behavior. For example, it is completely inappropriate to offer to pay for your dinner when you have been invited as a guest to a friend's home. It is equally inappropriate not to offer to pay for your dinner in a restaurant. The very same behavior takes on different meanings depending on the context.[1]

For this reason, it is useful to take up the question of the ethical use of incentives in very different contexts. Sensitivity to context increases the complexity of the issues but never in exactly the same ways in every case. Despite this diversity, the controversies in each case revolve around the same central questions identified in the last chapter on evaluating incentives.

Plea Bargaining

Amendment VI of the Constitution of the United States begins: "In *all* criminal prosecutions, the accused *shall enjoy* the right to a speedy and public trial" (my emphasis). Nonetheless, less than 10 percent of felony prosecutions actually go to trial. The other 90–95 percent are settled by a plea of guilty by the defendant.[2] Plea bargaining occurs when a defendant agrees to plead guilty in exchange for some consideration from the state, generally a reduced charge, a reduced sentence, or both. Plea bargaining is at the heart of our criminal justice system.

That was not always the case. While plea bargaining developed as informal practice during the late nineteenth century, it was officially prohibited for quite some time. In 1877, the Wisconsin Supreme Court declared that plea bargaining "was hardly, if at all distinguishable in principle from a direct sale of justice."[3] It was only in 1970 that the Supreme Court upheld the constitutionality of plea bargaining.[4] At first, it was justified in terms of deserved punishment: a defendant who admitted his guilt was said to deserve leniency. Today, plea bargaining is more often defended in terms of efficiency, and a plea bargain is considered legitimate so long as the defendant's plea is "voluntary and intelligent."[5]

The strongest contemporary defenders of plea bargaining explicitly rest their case on the premise that plea bargaining is indistinguishable in principle from any other kind of bargaining, contract, or market transaction.[6] Its opponents stress the disproportionate power relations between the prosecutor and the defendant as well as the distinctive purposes of the criminal jus-

tice system.[7] The controversy over plea bargaining is thus a perfect arena for examining one of the central claims of this book:
viewing incentives as a form of power, and not exclusively as a
form of trade, radically alters ethical judgments about them.

Defenders of plea bargaining view the practice as a form of
dispute settlement that closely resembles negotiations in civil
cases. Both parties avoid the risk of losing at trial: "Each party
trades the possibility of total victory for the certainty of avoid-
ing total defeat."[8] In addition, the prosecutor gains a conviction
without the effort and expense required to prove the defendant's
guilt in court, while the defendant gains a lighter sentence than
would be imposed if he were found guilty after a trial. Both
parties to the agreement are happier than they would be if they
were not permitted to strike the bargain. What could be wrong
with a system such as this?

The ethical claim behind this "marketplace" defense of plea
bargaining is that it protects freedom by protecting choice. The
right to contract or to exchange entitlements should not be restricted without good reason. Plea bargaining respects the autonomy of the parties. In particular, the criminal defendant is
clearly better off with the option to consider a plea bargain than
he would be without it. The high rate of guilty pleas testifies to
the fact that defendants believe that they are better off accepting the deals they are offered. From this point of view, critics of
plea bargaining appear paternalistic, that is, unwilling to allow
defendants to decide what is in their own best interests and willing to restrict their freedom "for their own good."

The central ethical challenge for this defense is to show that
plea bargains are, in fact, voluntary transactions that represent
legitimate contracts. Defenders acknowledge, drawing on contract law, that contracts are illegitimate where duress or fraud
is involved. Extensive philosophic discussions of what counts
as coercion are also brought to bear on the question of whether
plea bargaining is voluntary. One common starting point is to
argue that threats are coercive, but offers cannot be. The central
difference between the two is that if you reject an offer, you are

no worse off than before the offer was made. For example, a destitute person offered a large sum of money for her kidney may be sorely tempted, but she is not coerced. If she refuses the offer, she is no worse off than before. On the other hand, if a gunman threatens, "Your money or your life," either choice leaves you worse off than at your "baseline," before you ran into the gunman.[9]

The situation of the criminal defendant appears, at first glance, to resemble the first example rather than the second. If she rejects the offer of a reduced charge or a reduced sentence, she will stand trial, just as before. So long as her "baseline" is understood as her condition post-arrest, not pre-arrest, she will not be worse off for having rejected the offer. But given that there is a plea bargaining system, judges are often especially severe on defendants who reject a prosecutor's offer.* This makes the line between "threat" and "offer" very difficult to draw. They appear to be two sides of the same coin.[10] In effect, the message is, "Accept this offer of leniency and plead guilty, or we will 'throw the book at you.'" This formula exactly describes the situation dealt with in a 1970 Supreme Court decision on plea bargaining. The defendant, Hayes, had been indicted for forgery and was told that the prosecutor would recommend a five-year sentence in exchange for a guilty plea. If he rejected the offer, the prosecutor would seek an *additional* indictment under the Kentucky Habitual Criminals Act, where conviction would lead to life imprisonment. Hayes chose his right to trial, was convicted, and sentenced to life in prison. In upholding his conviction, the Supreme Court essentially held that there is no distinction between offers and threats in the plea bargaining context.[11]

A more promising approach to the question, called the "rights-violating" approach, argues that consent is invalidated, consent

---

*That judges are known to impose stiffer sentences on those who reject a plea agreement is called "implied plea bargaining."

is coerced, when a person is threatened with violation of his rights unless he chooses X and he has no reasonable alternative choice. This is why, confronted with a choice between his money or his life, the victim who chooses the "money" option clearly does not act voluntarily.[12] But in the case of plea bargaining, the prosecutor *does* have the right to take the defendant to trial. In plea bargaining, the prosecutor offers to forego the trial if the defendant will enter a guilty plea and accept a lighter sentence. The prosecutor is actually increasing the defendant's options by offering leniency. A defendant who accepts such an offer *is* acting voluntarily.[13]

Plea bargaining is not a coercive practice per se; the standard of voluntariness can be met. But prosecutors have a great deal of discretion, and practices resembling fraud are possible. A prosecutor can begin by overcharging defendants and then offer to reduce the charge. She can "bluff" as to the strength of her case (particularly because the laws governing discovery of evidence are not favorable to defendants at this stage of the criminal process). It should also be remembered that the negotiation takes place between the prosecutor and the defense attorney. The defendant sometimes has as little as twenty minutes to decide whether or not to accept a negotiated plea.[14] If consent needs to be not only voluntary but also fully informed, there is certainly cause for concern.

Moreover, there are ethical issues here beyond voluntariness. For example, large sentence differentials, like the difference Hayes faced between five years and life imprisonment, are a source of significant pressure on defendants to plead guilty.[15] And prosecutors are most likely to offer large charge or sentence reductions when they do *not* have a strong case, which is to say, when the defendant is most likely to be innocent. One case, often cited in the literature, involves a man charged with kidnaping and rape who was offered the opportunity to plead guilty to simple battery. His defense attorney believed he was innocent and advised him that conviction at trial was highly improbable, to which the defendant replied, "I can't take the chance."[16] And, of course, when the death penalty is a possibility, the pressure is extreme.[17]

For all of these reasons, plea bargaining, *in practice*, does not fit the picture of the standard market transaction or contract. And the defendant's choice in accepting a plea bargain would be difficult to describe as a meaningful expression of autonomy.[18]

The efficiency of the plea bargaining system is the second claim that justifies plea bargaining in the eyes of its defenders. Plea bargaining sets the "price" of crime, just like other kinds of markets set prices, and it should do so in a manner that secures the greatest degree of deterrence with the expenditure of the least amount of resources. Efficiency should result from a rational and free bargaining process. But aspects of the system can "skew" the bargain. For example, both prosecutors and defense attorneys have personal and professional interests that may influence their negotiating decisions in ways that depart from the interests of the state and the defendant, respectively. And defendants are unlikely to be making rational calculations of their interests. Psychological studies show that people's decisions are skewed in certain ways in high-risk situations.[19]

But there are deeper problems here. We don't really know what it means for a plea bargain to be "skewed" because we don't know what decision in a plea bargaining case is optimal. What is, for example, the effect of plea bargained punishments on deterrence? It might be that a system that appears as arbitrary and inconsistent as this one *undermines* deterrence. Moreover, while the prosecutor is thinking only about saving the costs of going to trial, there are many other costs to consider: for example, the costs of having a potentially dangerous criminal on the streets and the costs of incarceration. Oddly, in the debate over plea bargaining, consideration of costs always seems to be limited to the costs of the trial itself.

Finally, the system is meant to serve two purposes: to separate the guilty from the innocent and to determine appropriate punishment. While the second may be efficiently accomplished by plea bargaining understood according to a market model, the first is not. In a market situation or a civil suit, if a negotiated solution is not reached or if the case goes to trial, that is considered a failure. But in the context of criminal proceedings, it should not be considered a failure if the prosecutor does not offer a sweet enough deal to an innocent person and the case goes to trial. Is it a failure of the system when an innocent person pleads "not guilty"? On the contrary, this certainly ought to be the preferred result. And contrariwise, when a negotiated agreement *is* reached but the defendant is innocent, the system has failed.[20]

Defenders of plea bargaining, recognizing many of these problems with the current system, advocate various measures for reform: limits on sentence differentials, a new pay structure for defense attorneys, new rules of discovery, less prosecutorial discretion, and so forth.[21] Many critics of plea bargaining are also reformers, believing either that plea bargaining is inevitable or that the costs of abolishing the system are too high.[22]

But there are opponents of plea bargaining who argue that nothing short of abolition will do: plea bargaining is inherently unethical and irrational. These critics reject the analogy between plea bargaining and dispute settlements in civil cases, or between plea bargaining and market transactions. There are many differences. In civil cases, there are extensive opportunities for discovery of evidence, lawyers' fees are tied to the terms of the settlement, and so forth.[23] But most important, in criminal cases, the defendant and the prosecutor are not on a par with one another. This is not a dispute between two citizens but between a citizen and the society as a whole. The defendant is subject to the power of the state, and the prosecutor holds all of the cards. The prosecutor risks a lost conviction by going to trial; the defendant risks loss of liberty or even life. The situation for the defendant is "inherently coercive"; he or she is likely to be in pre-trial detention already, for example. And the defendant is likely to be poor and young. Recognizing the power relations in this situation, critics of plea bargaining are apt to question whether the defendant *can be* in a position to act voluntarily. Critics, like defenders, focus a good deal of energy on arguments over voluntariness.

But the fundamental issue, I believe, is not voluntariness but the purposes of the criminal justice system.[24] The system is meant to ascertain the facts according to the evidence and to assign punishment proportionate to the crime for the sake of protecting the public. These purposes—truth and justice—cannot be served by a bargaining process. In fact, a bargaining process necessarily undermines both. For this reason, the focus on voluntariness is not just misplaced emphasis, it is fundamentally misguided. If plea bargaining fails the "purposes" test, voluntariness need not even arise as an issue.[25]

With respect to justice, one critic likens plea bargaining to a professor who negotiates with his students over grades. The professor avoids the effort of grading papers by agreeing with the student that the student will accept a "B," foregoing both the chance of getting an "A" and the risk of getting a "C" if the professor has to read the paper.[26] Another commentator suggests that plea bargaining to determine sentences is like playing checkers to determine salaries.[27]

In assigning punishment, people are meant to get what they deserve. Guilt is like glory; disputed claims of either must be settled on the merits: "Just as you may not alienate the credit you deserve, you may not alienate the blame you deserve. We do not allow you to contract with someone to serve your jail term in your behalf or even to pay your criminal fine in your behalf. (No insurance for crimes allowed!)"[28] So here is another important difference between criminal proceedings and civil disputes.

A plea bargain always gives the defendant either more or less than she deserves and is therefore, *in principle*, an inappropriate means toward the end of meting out justice. Either the defendant is guilty but gets off easy by copping a plea, or the defendant is innocent but pleads guilty to avoid the risk of greater punishment. To make matters worse, punishment is distributed inequitably, with similar individuals who have committed the same crime in similar circumstances ending up with very different sentences, either because they were offered different deals or because one exercised his right to trial and the other did not.[29]

Similarly, plea bargaining fails the cause of truth. Plea bargains settle the question of guilt without adjudication of the evidence. Prosecutors also routinely charge defendants not with the crimes they actually committed but with crimes carrying lesser sentences. Completely convinced of the analogy between criminal cases and civil disputes, one defender of plea bargaining wonders why the court even bothers to assure itself that a guilty plea is supported by evidence of guilt.[30] From the perspective of the critics, this seems like a very odd question indeed. Yet, Rule 11 of the Federal Rules of Criminal Procedure governing plea bargaining contains a curious escape clause. The court must ascertain that the plea is voluntary and "did not result from force, threats or promises (*other than the promise in a plea agreement*)" (my emphasis). Perhaps we do not care that much about the truth of the matter after all.

Because plea bargaining undermines the purposes of the criminal justice system, it undermines its legitimacy. And this has an impact on the institutional culture within which lawyers and judges operate. It raises the "character" question. In a detailed account, a former defense attorney and prosecutor describes the differences in workplace norms between a county where judges routinely punished defendants and attorneys for bringing a case to trial and a county where they did not. In the first county, the corrupting power of the workgroup was evident; a culture of laziness developed among attorneys; defense attorneys sought to spend as little time as possible with their difficult clients; and the administration of justice became a matter of hustling.[31] Plea bargaining leads prosecutors and judges to act like "gunmen and blackmailers."[32]

When the legitimacy of the system is undermined, the effects ripple through the society. Anyone having contact with the criminal justice system is affected. A victim of a crime that could be described as kidnaping and assault with a deadly weapon is left bitterly cynical when his assailant is caught and charged with simple robbery, which puts him back on the streets in a few months. People living in high-crime communities, which may have the greatest contact with the police and prosecutors, become distrustful and disaffected. This is not a trivial consideration in judging the ethics of plea bargaining. Just as you have a right to vote, which you may waive but not sell, you have a right to a jury trial, which you may waive but should not be permitted to sell. To sell your vote undermines the integrity of the electoral system. To sell your guilty plea in exchange for leniency undermines the integrity of the criminal justice system.[33]

Actually, the focus of the matter probably should be reversed. Rather than look to the defendant, the "seller," we should look to the state, the "buyer." Is it legitimate for the state to offer to buy a guilty plea? Is this a legitimate incentive? Since most of the controversy over plea bargaining centers on the question of voluntariness, the focus of discussion is the defendant and even his interior condition: What pressures is he under? Is he acting rationally? Is he happier with the offer than he would be without it? When attention turns to the question of the purposes served by the criminal justice system, the focus shifts to the power and authority of the state: What is the responsibility of the state in the administration of criminal justice? Is plea bargaining an abuse of state power?[34]

Here, the legal doctrine of "unconstitutional conditions" is instructive. In some cases, though not always, the courts have prohibited government from offering benefits with certain kinds of "strings attached," that is, benefits that require a person to waive a constitutional right. The state cannot, for example, offer tax or unemployment benefits only to those who take a loyalty oath or offer employment opportunities only to those willing to work on Saturday. Such conditions infringe upon free speech and freedom of religion and are considered "unconstitutional conditions." In plea bargaining, the state's offer of leniency goes only to those willing to waive their right to trial by jury, their right to confront their accusers, and their right against self-incrimination. Whether or not the doctrine of "unconstitutional conditions" ought to apply to plea bargaining is a matter worth considering. Some have argued that "any fair view of the doctrine of unconstitutional conditions requires the condemnation of plea bargaining."[35] In their view, plea bargaining allows the state to evade its constitutional responsibilities.

The core of the critical argument is clear. The state has instituted a system of plea bargaining, presumably for the sole purpose of expediting the processing of criminal cases. But plea bargaining undermines the primary purposes of the criminal justice system; it cannot serve either truth or justice. Understood in this light, there is nothing paternalistic about the critique of plea bargaining. The defendant always has a right to choose to waive his Sixth Amendment right to trial, but he does not have a right to sell it—not because he cannot decide for himself where his interests lie but because it is an abuse of the power of the state to offer to buy it.

Does this mean that plea bargaining is never justified? I believe that this analysis allows for the legitimacy of one type of plea bargaining: plea bargaining for information. Bargaining for information occurs when the prosecutor offers leniency to a criminal "small fish" in exchange for information that will help the prosecutor apprehend and convict his "large fish" associates. Of course, the "small fish" gets less punishment than he deserves. But that is a small price to pay for the apprehension and punishment of more dangerous people. This sort of bargain serves the proper purposes of the system: uncovering evidence and punishing the guilty in order to protect society from criminal behavior.

Finally, we need to ask whether the abolition of plea bargaining is a practical possibility. We don't really know. There are certainly countries that function without it. In civil law countries, prosecutors often do not have the power to drop or reduce charges, and such systems often have no concept of a plea—a confession is simply entered into evidence and becomes part of the full consideration of the case. Alaska banned plea bargaining for a period of ten years. The few studies that have been done on the matter show that abolishing plea bargaining does not greatly increase the number of cases that go to trial. A significant number of defendants plead guilty *without* being offered anything in exchange.[36]

With respect to this question, there is a provocative comparison to be made between plea bargaining today and torture in medieval Europe. Both determine guilt without adjudication of the evidence. Plea bargaining arose as standard practice as the legal requirements for conducting a fair trial became more demanding. Torture arose when the testimony of two eyewitnesses became required for conviction at trial. Such a strict standard meant that guilt would be almost impossible to establish without a confession, coerced or otherwise. Coerced confessions under torture became the norm, regulated by various legal standards and practices.[37] Just as today it appears impossible to abolish plea bargaining in America as an integral part of the criminal justice system, I am sure there was a time when the abolition of torture in Europe appeared to be impossible as well.

Recruiting Medical Research Subjects

Modern medical research requires the participation of large numbers of people, healthy and sick, to study the effects of new medications before they can be put into general use. Such studies provide critically important public benefits, and for this reason, protocols that make it unlikely that research will take place, due to a shortage of subjects, carry an ethical burden. But are incentives an appropriate tool to recruit these participants—and, if they are, what *kinds* of incentives are appropriate?[38]

Although almost everyone uses medications at one time or another, there is relatively little public awareness of the controversy surrounding the ethics of recruiting subjects for the studies that make those medications possible. Among medical professionals, however, the matter has been hotly debated for years. Their sensitivity to the ethical questions can be explained, in part, as a reaction to the history of horrific abuses in research studies and experiments, particularly in research on "captive populations" such as prisoners and orphans. But quite apart from this history, there is an ethical issue at the center of medical research on human subjects that cannot be avoided, no matter how well the research is conducted: the research itself treats a person as if he or she were an object, a "thing"—like a piece of laboratory equipment or a guinea pig (though many people question whether even guinea pigs should be treated like "guinea pigs").

This issue is sometimes clouded by the choice of words used to describe the situation. "Research participants" or "participants in a study" sound like active agents with a certain dignity. "Subjects of medical experiments" are passive beings who will be acted upon by others. The latter language makes the ethical problem more apparent.

The problem seems to be easily addressed if research subjects are recruited as volunteers. Ideally, volunteers are those who would willingly join in the research enterprise and be highly motivated to contribute to the progress of medicine. Volunteers like these resemble scientists in days gone by who first experimented with their innovative treatments on themselves. Because the volunteers have willingly adopted the purpose of the research as their own, they retain their dignity even when they become subjects of experimentation.[39] This was the traditional view: *only* volunteers should be used as medical research subjects.

But what if there are not enough volunteers? Today, the demand for research subjects is rising due to policies requiring the inclusion of a wider range of demographic groups in research (e.g., women, children, racial minorities) as well as policies requiring that industry sponsor clinical research in order to get approval for marketing certain products. The growing need to recruit subjects makes the issue of incentives increasingly pressing, and the ethics of using incentives to recruit research subjects is being reevaluated.

There are only three alternatives to create a supply to meet the new demand: voluntary participation (persuasion), wages and incentives of all kinds (bargaining), and required participation—like jury duty or military service (coercion).[40] But there are settled norms against coerced participation in research that are unlikely to be challenged, so I leave this possibility aside.[41] And we can safely assume for our purposes here that volunteers alone will not be sufficient to fill the need for research subjects, particularly for healthy subjects. This means that the question of how incentives might be ethically employed is a crucial one.[42]

In practice, various forms of research participation are operating in the current system, much like firefighting, where there are volunteer firefighters, volunteer firefighters who receive incentives such as pension plans, and professional firefighters. Similarly, some research subjects are volunteers, some receive incentives such as free medical treatment, and some are paid enough to use participation in medical research as a source of income. Looking just at incentives for participation, the range of benefits can include reimbursement for the costs of participating, extra medical services, and cash incentives of varying amounts for completing different kinds of studies. It also has been suggested that being a research subject is a form of work that should be compensated with the going wage rate for unskilled labor;[43] in this view, it is unethical *not* to pay research participants. There are advantages and disadvantages to each of these approaches, but only cash incentives and wages are controversial.[44]

We know that there are ethical questions that arise with the use of incentives per se. There are also ethical questions that arise in human subjects research generally. The task here is to combine the two sets of concerns in order to establish ethical criteria for evaluating the use of incentives in human subjects research.

There are certain settled norms regarding the ethics of human subjects research. For example, requirements typically include review by a group distinct from the investigator to ensure that benefits to the public from the research are maximized, the risks to the research subjects are minimized, and informed consent is obtained for most research prior to participation. Much can be learned about the principles underlying these norms and practices by analyzing medical ethics codes.

In 1979, the National Commission for the Protection of Human Subjects of Biomedical and Behavioral Research issued its landmark Belmont Report. According to this report, three ethical principles are prima facie binding in considering research: beneficence, respect for persons, and justice—three criteria that correspond roughly to legitimacy of purpose, voluntariness, and fairness.

Beneficence implies that risks to subjects are minimized and that benefits of the research are maximized. The principle of beneficence can determine whether a particular research project may be ethically permissible, separable from consent. That is, certain research ought not to be done simply because the risks involved are not proportionate to the potential benefits, regardless of whether people are willing to participate.

Respect for persons derives from the philosophical principle of autonomy and the political principle of liberty, especially in its negative sense—the right to be left alone. Informed consent policies are one illustration of respect for persons: individuals who are asked to participate in research are given relevant information about the research, in a manner they can understand, before they authorize their participation. Voluntariness is at the heart of such consent. Here is the language of the report:

> An agreement to participate in research constitutes a valid consent only if voluntarily given. This element of informed consent requires conditions free of coercion and undue influence. Coercion occurs when an overt threat of harm is intentionally presented by one person to another in order to obtain compliance. Undue influence, by contrast, occurs through an offer of an excessive, unwarranted, inappropriate

or improper reward or other overture in order to obtain compliance. Also, inducements that would ordinarily be acceptable may become undue influences if the subject is especially vulnerable.

Unjustifiable pressures usually occur when persons in positions of authority or commanding influence—especially where possible sanctions are involved—urge a course of action for a subject. A continuum of such influencing factors exists, however, and it is impossible to state precisely where justifiable persuasion ends and undue influence begins. But undue influence would include actions such as manipulating a person's choice through the controlling influence of a close relative and threatening to withdraw health services to which an individual would otherwise be entitled.[45]

While considerations of respect for persons tend to focus on consent, a broader notion of respect for persons would also incorporate the need to treat participants in research with dignity. For example, the World Medical Association states the following in its Declaration of Helsinki: "It is the duty of the physician in medical research to protect the life, health, privacy, and dignity of the human subject."[46]

Finally, the Belmont Report's third principle, "justice," demands that individual research subjects be selected fairly and that appropriate populations are selected as research subjects. Because historical abuses of research subjects tended to occur among those who were in some way disadvantaged or vulnerable, justice in the selection of subject populations was typically understood as the need to protect such populations from inclusion in research. However, justice has come to be understood in some situations as fairness in access to the benefits of participating in research, for individuals and for groups. AIDS activists in the 1980s offered powerful arguments for access to potentially life-saving but experimental drugs. And it is now recognized that an overprotective stance toward "vulnerable" research participants could lead to serious inequities in the availability of medical treatment. If, for example, a drug is not tested with children, there can be dangerous ignorance of its clinical impact given their body size and development; or, if a heart medication is only tested in men, its efficacy for women will remain unknown. As a consequence, there are now multiple policies of governmental and professional groups requiring the inclusion of various population subgroups in research.[47] Beginning then, with the three established norms guiding human subjects research (beneficence, respect for persons, and justice), the question becomes whether using incentives in research ought to alter ethical judgments in any of these areas.

One of the prime considerations for whether research meets the test of beneficence is whether it involves a reasonable level of risk in relation to the prospect of benefit. If the risks are unreasonable, it would be unethical to ask anyone to take them, regardless of whether they are asked to volunteer or offered wages or incentives. On the other hand, suppose there is an authoritative determination that a research project involves reasonable risks in relation to benefits. In this case, offering incentives to recruit subjects would not change that judgment or raise ethical problems.

A problem would arise, however, if the use of incentives were allowed to influence the determination of risk in the first place, that is, if the scientists were released from the responsibility of making an independent judgment on the merits and instead based their risk assessment on what people were willing to do for gain—as if risks that people are willing to take for gain are ipso facto reasonable because they are acceptable to the doer. But the same logic would apply to volunteers as well: just because people are willing to take unreasonable risks does not mean that they ought to be invited to do so. Thus, with respect to the principle of beneficence at least, incentives are not a factor in the ethical equation.

The situation is altogether different when we turn to respect for persons in the form of autonomy. Here there is an intersection between the requirement that research subjects be recruited without "coercion or undue influence" and the concern that incentives can be manipulative in a variety of ways. Where exactly is that intersection?

It is not at the point of bribery or of blackmail. Incentives in medical research induce people to do something inherently good (assuming of course that the research is necessary, sound in design, and conducted with integrity), not to violate their duties. So they are not bribery. Neither are they blackmail, since incentives are offers and not threats; one can refuse them and remain no worse off than before.[48] Those who see a problem with incentives in this area claim that incentives, particularly relatively large incentives, are a form of coercion, undue influence, or undue inducement.

This is by far the most prominent issue in the discussion over the ethics of incentives for recruiting research subjects. It is widely believed that incentives can be too large, constituting "irresistible" or "coercive" offers, and that such offers violate the ethical requirement of voluntary consent.[49] For quite some time now, this claim has been debated without much apparent motion in the debate. Over twenty years ago, Ruth Macklin and Lisa Newton locked horns over the issue with arguments very similar to those canvassed in a recent article on the ethics of offering incentives to the homeless for participation in drug studies.[50]

On one hand, those who criticize incentives as undue inducements argue that an offer can be irresistibly attractive.[51] A destitute person may be induced to do something against his better judgment, and even almost against his will, by the offer of a large amount of money, for example. Such an offer is so close to coercion—operating essentially "against his will"—that it might as well be coercion given the circumstances. Thus, researchers ought to be particularly wary of offering incentives to vulnerable populations since this practice can be unethical.

On the other hand, the critics of this view characterize it as paternalistic, arguing that to say that an offer is irresistibly attractive is simply to say that the person accepting the offer desired to have the thing offered more than anything else. How can this be characterized as anything other than a free choice? There are, in this view, no such things as undue inducements. What people really object to in these situations is not the incentive but the fact of inequality that leads some people to choose differently than others. Given the existence of the inequality, it is a paternalistic infringement of liberty to deny destitute people the opportunity to make choices that we are perfectly willing to offer to wealthier people only because we are afraid that the poor will make the "wrong" choice. From this perspective, to fail to offer incentives is unethical to the extent that it is a deprivation of liberty.[52]

The debate—as long as it remains in this form—is unresolvable because the positions arise out of irreconcilable paradigms. The argument that incentives maximize choice and therefore maximize freedom arises from the economic paradigm according to which an incentive is simply one form of trade. The alternative argument that incentives can constitute undue influence evaluates incentives as one form of power.

Resolving the dilemma requires acknowledging the element of truth in both positions. The proponents of incentives are certainly correct that it is a voluntary action when a very poor person agrees to participate in research in exchange for a large sum of money. But those who characterize this sort of choice as an undue inducement also have a point. The problem in this debate is the focus on the question of the degree of voluntariness or coercion, as if that were the only ethical question. Greater light can be shed by focusing instead on the other ethical dimensions of the problem.

Some examples may serve to clarify the issues. Many people would find nothing problematic in offering free sterilization procedures in a situation in which overpopulation was a problem. But those same people might very well worry about large monetary incentives to encourage people to take advantage of those services. At the same time, there is little protest in countries where tax breaks are given to parents of large families to encourage population growth, though if there were huge cash payments, ethical concerns might surface. What explains this series of judgments? In the case of sterilization, the concern might be that a large monetary incentive could induce people to take a serious, permanent step that they will later regret. The large incentive may compromise the person's ability to rationally weigh short-term and long-term consequences.[53] Moreover, one might wonder whether it is ethically appropriate to put a price on the possibility of having a family. It matters what the incentive offer is about. In the case of tax incentives for large families, the concern is that *huge* cash awards might serve as inducements to people who don't really want children, with obvious implications for the welfare of such children. It is important to do some things for the right reasons, and money is not always one of those reasons.

In general, then, while incentives are always employed to induce someone to do what they otherwise might not, the ethically suspect incentive is one used to induce someone to do something to which they are strongly averse, particularly if the aversion is a principled one or a matter of moral scruple.[54] This is the kind of manipulation, pressure, or seduction captured in the colloquial phrase "against my better judgment."[55] A choice that involves an aversion is different, for example, from the choice between one car and another when I already have decided that I want to buy a car. To deliberately induce religious people to work on the Sabbath by offering large incentives would involve an attempt to get them to act against what they see as their duties; it would be a form of bribery.[56]

The point can be illustrated with examples from medical research. In the now infamous hepatitis experiments conducted at the Willowbrook State School, parents were encouraged to enlist their mentally disabled children in a research project requiring the children to be infected with hepatitis.[57] The incentive was an offer of a place for the child in a residential treatment facility that otherwise would be difficult to secure. Apart from the ethical problem of the apparent unfairness of allowing some families to jump the queue, the incentive was entirely inappropriate. These parents were reluctant to allow their children to participate in this research out of a laudable concern for their children. The incentive can be seen as an attempt to manipulate this very concern for their children's welfare to overcome their reluctance to participate.[58]

Consider the question of whether incentives ought to be offered to pregnant women to become research subjects. All other things being equal, the answer should certainly be "no." To encourage women to put their children at risk in exchange for cash is a kind of bribe, a temptation to violate their primary responsibility. But, on the other hand, if there are no studies done on pregnant women, there will be no knowledge of how to treat them when they are sick nor medications to use for treatment.[59] The matter is one of balancing considerations of character and undue influence with considerations of purpose. And the balance may be struck differently depending on the particularities of the proposed study: How risky is it to the mother and the fetus? How important are the results likely to be for saving lives? Could the research subject benefit from the study itself? And so on.

This sort of analysis, which considers what the study involves and not just the size of the incentive, has important implications for the ethics of "completion bonuses" as well. A bonus for completing an innocuous research study (e.g., filling out a simple questionnaire on several separate occasions) poses no ethical problems. But if the research is painful, debilitating, or distressing for the subject (e.g., repeated biopsies), a completion bonus can be seen as undue influence not because it is the same as coercion but because it is an attempt to overcome the subject's reasonable resistance to what he or she is being asked to suffer. Every major code of ethics for research with human subjects contains the provision that participants ought to have the right to exit at any time. The ease of voluntary exit from a research study is an important check on the researcher's judgment as to what is a reasonable level of risk or cost to the research subject. A deliberate attempt to structure incentives so as to overcome reasonable aversions that ought to be respected negates that check.

Respect for persons thus requires respect for certain of their values, beliefs, and judgments. It requires refraining from making seductive offers—offers that *ought* to be resisted in some sense.

There is a second sort of undue influence, which involves trading on power in one sphere to influence outcomes in another, that also has some relevance to our question. For example, consider the situation where a professor gives medical students extra credit for agreeing to participate as subjects in her research. Assuming that their participation has no educational value, this is undue influence because grades, which should reflect learning in the course, are being given for a different purpose. The professor is using her legitimate authority to grade students' work on its merits to secure an entirely unrelated benefit for herself. If the currency is grades, both the teacher and the students receive benefits they do not rightly deserve. It would be better ethically to offer money in these circumstances in order to separate the incentive from the teacher's academic authority. Better still would be to avoid having teachers use their own students as research subjects.[60] Respect for persons in human subjects research requires care to avoid exploiting people in dependent positions, whether students or patients.

The principle of respect for persons in research also requires that research subjects be treated with dignity, and here, too, the use of incentives can exacerbate the ethical problem. Many medical practices involve undignified procedures, embarrassing situations, and degrading experiences. They can be physically invasive, upset the customary boundaries of privacy, or involve areas of the body generally associated with feelings of shame. People voluntarily, though often reluctantly, tolerate these sorts of indignities when they believe them to be necessary for health care. In the context of medical research, subjects may be required to overcome their usual inhibitions for the sake of the research.

To volunteer to undergo undignified procedures for altruistic reasons might be considered a particularly noble action.

But how does offering incentives to participate affect the ethical picture? At the very least, it introduces a twofold concern for dignity: that researchers will consider themselves freer to treat "recompensed" individuals in degrading ways and that a regime of payments for objectified uses of the body might erode the collective respect for personal dignity in the culture.[61] This is a complex issue, but it is important to put it on the table.

Finally, I turn to the question of the principle of justice as it requires fairness in the selection of research subjects. Today there is a trend toward considering justice to mean fair access to opportunities to participate in research rather than as the protection of participants from exploitation. But the use of incentives raises some distinct questions under both conceptions of justice.

Conceiving of justice as protection from exploitation assumes that vulnerable persons need to be protected from the risks of research. The notion of vulnerability in the context of research is quite broad and incorporates a variety of characteristics including the capacity to give consent, the presence of dependency relationships, and poverty. Incentives are simply inappropriate if a person is unable to weigh and evaluate them, and they can be considered an undue influence in situations of dependency relationships. Moreover, the issue of poverty is of special relevance when considering incentives. If researchers using incentives to recruit want to spend the least possible amount, they will be tempted to seek out poor and vulnerable populations—homeless people, for example. Increasingly, medical research subjects are recruited in developing countries. This practice is controversial, raising concerns about exploitation when the research is burdensome and the benefits are unlikely to accrue to the participating group.[62]

On the other hand, when the conception of justice centers on fair access to research opportunities, careful consideration needs to be given to including populations that might benefit from participation (either in the process of research itself or so that the results of the research will be useful for this population in the future). Powerful arguments justify the inclusion of a broad range of populations in research, although meeting these claims in practice can be challenging due to the need to recruit and retain persons who for historical or other reasons may be reluctant to participate in research. For example, there appears to be lingering distrust in the research enterprise among persons of color in the United States, a fact that some trace back to the historical abuse of African Americans in research (e.g., the U.S. Public Health Service Study of Syphilis that was conducted in Tuskegee, Alabama).[63] Accordingly, the need to use incentives to overcome barriers to recruitment in research among this population would not be surprising. However, important issues are raised about fairness when using incentives in this way. Would it be appropriate to have a differential use of incentives within a particular research project? To target incentives to persons otherwise unlikely to enroll and offer them greater incentives than other participants might meet the demands of access justice, but it does raise concerns about fairness for all participants. Why should some subjects receive an incentive when others do not? After all, we are generally sensitive about inequalities that we can see. There would likely be broad objections, for example, to paying richer people more if you needed their participation, or paying African Americans more if you particularly needed them to participate.* Whether the issue is protection from exploitation or inclusion in research, the question of fairness cannot be avoided.

To summarize: incentives can be used to recruit subjects in many situations without any ethical qualms where all other ethical criteria are met—that is to say, incentives *themselves* are not the ethical problem here generally speaking. If the research

---

*Differential payments and costs are not always considered unfair. Consider, for example, the different prices paid for airline seats on the same flight.

meets the usual ethical criteria for human subjects research, the introduction of incentives will generally be benign. Incentives become problematic when conjoined with the following factors, singly or in combination with one another: where the subject is in a dependency relationship with the researcher; where the research is degrading; or where the participant has a strong, principled aversion to the study. When these conditions are present, the use of incentives is highly questionable. And if a number of these conditions are present simultaneously, complexity obviously increases.

This means that there are clear cases but also many gray areas. I have tried to identify here the essential questions to ask and the essential factors to consider in reaching a determination in the gray areas. Sensitivity to these factors helps us see why teachers ought to avoid recruiting their own students as research subjects in return for better grades; why large completion bonuses where research is degrading or burdensome are suspect; why the use of incentives to recruit subjects for research involving religious or moral concerns ought to be carefully scrutinized; and so forth.

These are not clear-cut rules. They are guides for judgment, at most, but they do not leave us at a total loss. For example, consider the hypothetical case where cash incentives are offered through an advertisement in a high school newspaper for sexually active teenagers willing to participate in a research study. Some religious students object, viewing the incentives as a reward for immoral behavior. And one might imagine others objecting that it undermines the cultural support of teenage abstinence as an important value in a more general sense. But if the incentives offered were free treatment of sexually transmitted infections, counseling, or birth control, the picture could change considerably with respect to these concerns. There are multiple factors involved in assessing the propriety of any particular incentive program and difficult judgments to be made; sometimes, even attention to the kind of incentive that is offered can make an ethical difference.

The factors listed above and the kinds of judgments they require differ substantially from those considered crucial in most previous discussions of incentives as undue influence. That difference lies in the fact that this analysis does not view the ethical issue of undue influence as an issue of coercion. Believing coercion to be the issue leads to a misplaced emphasis on the *size* of the incentive. Consider the Belmont Report's condemnation of "excessive" incentives cited above.[64] But the size of the incentive is not important in itself. If a researcher were to offer $1,000 to a prospective participant to complete a psychological questionnaire, one would consider it a foolish incentive but certainly not unethical because "excessive" or "coercive."

Believing that the size of the incentive is the problem leads to a perverse result. Where the risks of a study are high, researchers avoid offering large incentives because they fear that they will unethically induce participation by making an irresistible offer. For this reason, research guidelines usually prohibit studies from offering higher payments to compensate for risk. But prospective participants generally assume that the level of risk and the level of payment are correlated—that higher payment is a signal of higher risk. Thus, if the payment is higher, they take greater pains to inform themselves of the risks. The process of informed consent may be improved by allowing incentives to rise when risks are higher.[65]

Large incentives only become problematic in the presence of the other sorts of factors that we have identified. Undue influence occurs when an incentive is attractive enough to tempt people to participate in a research study "against their better judgment." Thus, this analysis differs from others because it does not conclude either that large incentives ought to be rejected as coercive or that all incentives ought to be permitted as opportunities for free choice.

Of course, practical difficulties of implementation are inherent in this analysis. The need for large incentives can be a rough indicator that there may be an ethical concern that requires attention. We might say as a rule of thumb that if you cannot secure participation without offering large incentives or if only the indigent will agree to participate in your study and the incentives you are offering are comparable to studies drawing wider participation, the study probably produces strong aversions for one reason or another. It matters what the reason is. For researchers, this should be an immediate trigger for a careful ethical analysis.

I want to stress that most of the time for most research studies, the use of incentives to recruit and retain research subjects is entirely innocuous. But there are some areas where it is not. It follows that there will be some research studies that should not be done on account of ethics requirements with respect to incentives. So be it. The ethical responsibility to improve medical care must be balanced against the ethical responsibility to treat research subjects as autonomous individuals deserving of respect. Incentives used in an ethically appropriate manner can play an important role in striking that balance.

IMF Loan Conditions

In 1944, as part of the Bretton Woods Agreements, the International Monetary Fund (IMF) was founded to promote international financial stability by serving as an international lender that could help nations temporarily facing balance-of-payments problems and in need of credit. Countries that join the IMF (and today, the vast majority of countries are members) hold a specified amount of currency on reserve at the fund, and these funds provide a pool of resources for IMF lending. IMF loan "conditionality" is the practice of requiring governments to adopt certain policies and practices as a condition of receiving a loan. The government's desire for the loan becomes the motivation to fulfill its conditions. The "strings" attached to IMF loans make these agreements an interesting case for the investigation of the ethics of incentives.

Over time, the loan conditions have multiplied as the purposes of the IMF have changed and expanded.[66] Through the Latin

American debt crisis of the 1980s, the transitions in Eastern Europe toward market economies, and the East Asian financial crisis of the late 1990s, the IMF has moved far from the limited goal of solving temporary liquidity problems and toward the far broader goal of fostering sustained economic growth. The reasoning has been that repeated crises can be prevented and loans can be repaid only if nations fix their underlying economic problems. And that will happen, in turn, only if nations make significant political changes to increase accountability, reduce corruption, and ensure the rule of law. Consequently, loan conditions now include not only what are called "structural adjustments" (such as reducing budget deficits, raising taxes, raising interest rates, privatization, and trade liberalization) but also what are called "good governance" conditions.[67]

The conditions, or "strings," that the IMF attaches to its loans have been highly controversial. Similar controversies arise in discussions of foreign aid and World Bank programs, which also require economic and political adjustments. The major points of contention involve questions of voluntariness, undue influence, and particularly effectiveness—do these incentive programs do more harm than good?

Attaching conditions to loans or grants is widespread across many domains and is often not controversial in the least. Foundations giving grants to nonprofit organizations attach conditions to make sure that their money is used for its intended purpose, for example. The U.S. federal and state governments attach conditions to grants that support all kinds of organizations and activities. Why are such conditions sometimes ethically problematic and sometimes not?

Issues of voluntariness and purpose, efficacy and fairness, accountability and undue influence are all affected by the fact that both the IMF and the nation-state are complex entities. IMF loan conditionality is not like incentives between two individuals. The multinational IMF has responsibilities to its member states as well as to loan recipients. And all of the members are not equally powerful. The United States, for example, has been criticized for political manipulation of the fund—a form of undue influence.[68] Debtor nations are also composed of multiple actors. An agreement between the IMF and a nation's finance ministers may require implementation by a reluctant parliament, for example. And of course, the government is distinct from the people and a nation's elite is distinct from its lower classes. Those who consent to an IMF loan agreement are often not the same people as those who most feel the effects of its conditions.[69]

Moreover, we are considering ethical issues in the domain of international relations, and it is not clear that the same rules that apply to relations between individuals or to relations within nations apply here. Is respect for national sovereignty a fundamental principle analogous to respect for the dignity and autonomy of each individual? Or does respect for sovereignty need to give way at times, particularly when a sovereign government systematically violates the principle of respect for individual autonomy within its borders? Do nations and international organizations have an obligation to use their power for good or should they refrain from interfering? Or is the international arena one where "the strong do what they will, and the weak suffer what they must," as Thucydides' Athenian ambassadors proclaim?[70]

For all of these reasons, what might look like a straightforward and ethically benign contract is really a rather complicated matter. IMF agreements seem unproblematic: an IMF loan agreement is reached through a consensual process only after a member nation requests a loan from the fund; negotiations take place to settle terms and conditions; and the specifics are set out in a "Letter of Intent." What has made these agreements so controversial?

Not surprisingly, one question that arises is whether these agreements can be considered voluntary given that they are often made under duress. Nations approach the IMF as a "lender of last resort" when private capital is no longer forthcoming and their economies are in crisis. Of course, they are free to walk away from IMF negotiations, as President Nyerere of Tanzania did in the early 1980s.[71] But their extreme need and lack of alternatives create a situation where the IMF can exploit their weakness. The argument is one that we have seen before, both in discussing plea bargaining and in discussing human subjects research. Can we be satisfied that parties act voluntarily when there are large inequalities of power and resources between them and one party is in a desperate situation?

Critics view loan conditions as *imposed* by the IMF on debtor nations.[72] In their view, the fact that loan agreements set up sanctions for noncompliance implies that nations are not accepting those conditions voluntarily. They question why it is necessary to make the loans *conditional* on enacting the specified economic reforms if the government actually wants to undertake those reforms anyway. After all, the IMF could simply advise governments on policies that would help restore their economic health.

There is an answer to the critics' question that requires recognizing the many actors involved in this situation. Conditionality serves a number of purposes, most of which are only indirectly related to compliance. For example, a government may wish to enact austerity measures that they know will be unpopular. In this case, conditionality allows the government to use the IMF as a scapegoat, shifting the blame for the policies onto the fund. The government officials who have entered into the agreement with the IMF can use the agreement as leverage in securing support from other politicians who will go along with controversial policies rather than jeopardize the loan. In addition, the conditional loan agreement gives a credible signal to private financial institutions that the debtor country is on the way to economic health. For all of these reasons, a nation may accept conditions voluntarily.[73]

Moreover, some argue that IMF loan conditions are indeed imposed and that the IMF is well within its rights to impose them. Without conditionality, debtor nations will be tempted to irresponsibly avoid necessary, but painful, reforms, knowing that the IMF will always be there to bail them out as a "lender of last resort."[74] Conditionality provides the incentive for a government to change the behavior that created the problem in the first place, which will allow it eventually to repay the loan.

Let us suppose that the criterion of voluntariness is met in the sense that the government freely consents to accept loan conditions. We still need to be concerned with the distinction between the consent of the government and the consent of the people. And here, the question of voluntariness begins to blend with the question of undue influence. Who should be making decisions about a nation's economic policies? The critics charge the IMF with interfering with democratic political processes (where the debtor nations are democracies) and with acting where they have no authority to act—a classic charge of undue influence: "The legitimate political institutions of the country should determine the nation's economic structure and the nature of its institutions. A nation's desperate need for short-term financial help does not give the IMF the moral right to substitute its technical judgments for the outcomes of the nation's political process."[75]

Can democracy or popular participation be reconciled with economic policies dictated by outsiders? The question is sharply posed by situations like that in Brazil in 2003. President Lula had been elected on a platform of reducing poverty, and the IMF was requiring large budget surpluses, likely to exacerbate poverty, as part of its loan condition package.[76] The question is sometimes asked in terms of sovereignty more generally as well. In an article published in the *New York Times* concerning the financial difficulties of Greece, Portugal, Spain, Ireland, and Italy on February 5, 2010, the reporter wrote, "a bailout, if it comes, will raise the question of terms. How much political sovereignty will the bailed-out countries *be forced* to surrender?"[77] Some see the IMF interfering with sovereignty when its loan conditions specify policies that are usually determined by domestic political processes. Others argue that, on the contrary, it is a legitimate act of sovereignty for a government to enter into a binding international agreement.

The IMF is particularly vulnerable to charges of undue influence—acting beyond the bounds of its legitimate authority and thereby interfering with democracy and sovereignty—on account of the "mission creep" described earlier. As its mission has expanded from helping with short-term liquidity problems to encouraging growth, the conditions attached to its loans have become increasingly intrusive, both in the form of micromanagement and because they reach to central features of a nation's economy.[78] Reformers on both the left and the right have called for narrowing the scope of IMF action, both by restricting its purposes and by limiting the use of loan conditionality to certain kinds of cases.[79]

The IMF itself has responded with periodic reviews of conditionality principles and practices. The IMF recognizes that there are limits, in principle, to the use of its power. In recent official statements, it asserts that it employs conditionality only as a means to "safeguard the use of IMF resources." IMF policies address only economic, not political, aspects of a country's policies and practices. The IMF "should not be influenced by the nature of a political regime of a country, nor should it interfere with domestic or foreign politics of any member." The IMF has also stressed "ownership" and "streamlining conditionality" as guiding principles.[80] "Ownership" exists when a country is committed to the policies required as conditions of its loan and adopts them as its own goals. In other words, the more ownership there is, the less imposition there is. "Streamlining conditionality" involves using conditions "parsimoniously," reducing their number, and limiting their scope to measures "critical for achieving the program's macroeconomic objectives."[81]

The striking thing is that both the IMF and its critics seem to recognize that only certain sorts of "strings" are legitimate. The power that the IMF has because of its resources ought not to be used to extend its influence beyond the legitimate sphere of its authority, *even if the debtor nation freely accepts the conditions*. The problem is to define the legitimate purposes of IMF loan programs. How should the boundary of the IMF's proper sphere of influence be drawn?

The fund tries to draw a line between economic and political conditions, and it tries to limit its conditions to those critically necessary to achieve its economic purposes. Yet neither of these is a plausible limit-setting strategy. First, economic policy *is* political, certainly as soon as it affects matters of resource distribution. Tax and budget policies are never apolitical. Moreover, critics argue that the free market ideology that has governed IMF policy is itself a subject of major *political* debate and not a set of settled scientific truths that can be universally applied.[82]

Second, a limited purpose seems difficult to maintain in the face of a chain of logic whereby, in order to attain the limited goal of preventing future financial crises and ensuring loan repayment, major restructuring of the economy seems necessary. A large sphere of action is legitimated as instrumental to a nominally restricted purpose. Sustained growth becomes justified as the necessary prerequisite of ensuring financial stability. Once that step is taken, almost any social policy could be defended as "necessary"—education for girls, for example. The IMF is even considering environmental safety conditions attached to its loans, despite its rhetoric about limiting conditions to "necessary" and "critical" measures.[83]

But I suspect that the controversy over undue influence is as heated as it is not primarily because the IMF has overstepped the bounds of its authority but because the effects of its policies are highly controversial. If IMF loan conditionality programs clearly worked to produce sustained growth and alleviate poverty, there would be less concern, rightly or wrongly, with the issue of interference. The question of effectiveness is at the heart of this debate. Critics argue that it is unethical to increase the suffering of the world's poor and that the austerity measures demanded by IMF loan programs do exactly that. Moreover, it is unfair for the poor to bear the lion's share of the burden of restoring economic health when they bear no responsibility for the problem. Even their governments may bear less responsibility than at first appears. For example, the Latin American debt crisis was triggered by a change in interest rates in the United States, undertaken for domestic reasons.[84] Finally, the IMF itself is not accountable, either to debtor governments or to their people, when it gives bad advice or requires counterproductive measures that produce economic hardships with their attendant political instability.[85] IMF incentives are meant to benefit debtor nations, but who is to be the judge of whether or not they actually do?

These questions—do IMF loan conditions work and are they fair—cannot be answered without empirical knowledge of what the effects of IMF programs actually are. And it turns out that this is not an easy thing to discover, since it is not possible to know directly what the economic situation of a country would have been had it not received a conditional loan. Comparing countries that receive loans to countries that do not is also problematic because these two groups may differ systematically in other respects as well. Despite these difficulties, there is a consensus in the research literature that IMF programs tend to increase inequality within the country receiving the loan. Conclusions are tentative with respect to the impact of these programs on economic growth, but, in general, the results are unimpressive. Twenty years of studies show little or no impact on growth, while the most recent studies show negative impacts on growth.[86]

These conclusions support the contentions of IMF critics. But the controversy over IMF programs continues, in part because there is a disagreement over whether countries actually comply with loan conditions (discussed below) and in part because the entire argument is embedded in a larger debate over laissez-faire economic policies. Defenders of the IMF see the increased inequality as a short-term consequence of policies necessary to establish long-term growth that will benefit everyone. In their view, if growth has been disappointing, it is because laissez-faire policies have not been pursued aggressively enough.[87]

Finally, the controversy is embedded in yet another debate, one over global justice.[88] What do the powerful and rich owe to the powerless and poor internationally? How should powerful nations and international institutions use their power? We have already seen the argument that the IMF should not use loan conditionality to interfere with the sovereignty of debtor nations. But the argument is also made that the powerful have a responsibility to use their power to improve the situation of the weak—or at least to withdraw support from dictators. Lending money to tyrants lends support as well and implicates the lender in political evils. Making loans or foreign aid conditional on improvements in a nation's human rights record, for example, might be considered a more responsible approach. From this point of view, the political neutrality of the IMF is quite problematic. It seems that whereas it is sometimes unethical to attach "strings" to loans or foreign aid, it is sometimes unethical *not* to do so.[89]

By now it should be clear how complicated it is to reach a judgment about the ethics of incentives in this domain, both because of the number of issues involved and because the interactions take place between complex agents. But there is one more difficulty to consider. Participants in the general, public debate often seem to assume that the IMF is a very powerful institution and that by attaching "strings" it can virtually dictate the behavior of loan recipients. But there is reason to doubt that recipient countries can be controlled like puppets or that incentives are as effective as is often assumed.

Loan conditions are difficult to enforce, especially when the number of conditions multiplies, and sometimes the IMF is reluctant to enforce them for political reasons. Nations favored by the United States are less likely to face punishment for noncompliance, for example.[90] The IMF clearly believes that compliance rates have been low; this is one reason for pursuing a policy of increased "ownership" and for experimenting with ex ante conditionality, which requires certain actions before the loan is received. If compliance rates are indeed low, the argument of IMF defenders is strengthened. In this case, poor economic results cannot be attributed to the policies promoted by loan conditions.[91] Instead, greater compliance with those very conditions might solve the problem.

It is very difficult to measure compliance with loan conditions, and not a great deal is known about it. We do know that some conditions receive much greater compliance rates than others, varying between around 70 percent and around 30 percent.[92] We also know that the record of compliance with conditions attached to foreign aid and to loans from international financial institutions generally is not impressive.[93] I do not find this surprising. Who would really expect a dictatorial regime to alter its approach to human rights, for example, in exchange for development aid? I would not expect a democratic regime to make significant, long-term changes in response to short-term financial offers either, for that matter.

The IMF loan conditions controversy reveals a kind of exaggerated faith in the power of incentives to bring about change. The assumption is that if someone wants the benefit you have to offer, they will do what you require of them in order to receive that benefit. But this is too simple. The party receiving the benefit with "strings attached" is probably not infinitely malleable; some required changes may be simply out of reach, particularly within a limited time frame. And the relationship between the more powerful party and the less powerful one is still a relationship of interdependence. In some situations, the party holding the "strings" may have more to lose by enforcing conditions than by letting noncompliance go unpunished. The "powerful" party is not powerful in every respect, and neither is the "powerless" one entirely powerless. Reaching for incentive programs as a tool for solving complex problems often involves a failure to appreciate the limits of power.

Belief in the power of "strings" resembles the mentality of the "Planners," a term coined by William Easterly. Primary characteristics of the Planners' mentality include the following: they apply global blueprints; they think they already know the answers (although sitting at the "top," they have little knowledge of the "bottom"); they think that problems are technical and amenable to engineering solutions; and they believe outsiders know enough to impose those solutions. In Easterly's view, IMF loan conditionality is a perfect example of the failure of the Planners' approach.[94] In the terms employed in this book, it is a failure of incentives employed as a tool of social engineering.

Everyone involved in this controversy, on the left and the right, seems to think that IMF loan conditionality programs have failed in one way or another. Everyone also seems to agree that loan conditions are only ethically legitimate if certain procedural criteria are met: conditions must be voluntarily accepted and directly tied to the limited purposes of the fund. Conditionality is illegitimate where the IMF can be said to exploit the weakness of a member nation when, in times of financial crisis, it imposes policies and practices as loan conditions that properly ought to be determined by domestic political processes or that extend beyond what is necessary to repay the loan. Loan agreements must be voluntary and bounded by the proper sphere of IMF authority.

Moreover, even if these "procedural" conditions are met, we cannot judge loan conditionality to be ethically legitimate if the results of fulfilling the conditions harm people unfairly while providing little or no long-term benefit. The "substantive" effects of the loan conditions are part of the ethical judgment of their use. Both "procedural" and "substantive" questions must be asked in considering the ethics of loan conditionality, and asked by those with the "upper hand"—in this case, the IMF and its wealthiest member states. The question of the ethics of incentives in this domain, as always, is a question of the use and abuse of power.

Motivating Children to Learn

In Dallas, Chicago, Washington, D.C., and other urban areas, "pay for grades" programs have quickly become popular.* The programs vary in the age of students involved (from third grade to high school), in the behaviors rewarded (attendance, high test

---

*New York's program (privately funded) also included payments to parents for responsible behavior such as taking children to the dentist and holding down a job. The city canceled the program after three years because the results were unimpressive.

scores, high grades, basic classroom decorum), and in the pay-offs (one program allows students to earn up to $1,500). The hope is that these programs, generally targeting poor, minority students, will help solve the seemingly intractable problem of the minority "achievement gap." While it is very common to use incentives of various kinds to motivate children to do all kinds of things, paying cold, hard cash for good grades is particularly controversial.

In evaluating the ethics of "pay for grades" policies, the first obvious question is, "Do these programs work as compared to alternative approaches?" And, of course, some of the controversy swirls around the question of what it means for a program to "work"—are higher grades or better annual test scores sufficient to declare victory, or are we aiming for students who will continue to be motivated to learn in the future? So, the first question leads directly to the second: "How do these programs affect character?"

Of all of the incentive programs examined in this book, incentives used to motivate children to learn are most centrally involved with the character question. Schools, after all, are concerned not only with the cognitive development of children but also with their personal and social development; these are central to their purpose.[95] And the concern with character involves encouraging children not only to do the right things but also to do them for the right reasons.

The striking thing is that today's incentive programs are touted as radically innovative approaches where "the jury is out" on whether or not incentives work to motivate academic achievement.[96] In fact, there is nothing new about these sorts of programs—and the debate over their effectiveness is a very old one. Moreover, with fifty-plus years of research in psychology and contemporary work in economics, there seems to be a clear consensus about two conclusions. First, under certain circumstances, incentives "backfire," producing the opposite of their intended effects.[97] Second, monetary incentives "crowd out" less mercenary motives, producing a negative effect on character as well as on outcomes. Thus, incentives work sometimes to accomplish certain kinds of goals, and they fail at other times. The important thing, as we will see shortly, is that the research is clear about which conditions produce which results.

Disputes over motivation stand behind the controversies over incentives in education. How are incentives—a form of extrinsic motivation—related to intrinsic forms of motivation, such as the satisfaction of curiosity or the sense of competence or mastery? This question has been around for a very long time. Before it arose around paying cash for grades, it was disputed about the grades themselves. It is worth noting that paying for grades is offering an incentive for an incentive. Grades are an incentive to learn—an extrinsic reward for academic achievement—and "grade-grubbing" students have always been distinguished from those who learn primarily for learning's sake. Critics of grades have always been proponents of intrinsic motivation.

The psychologists' categories, "extrinsic" and "intrinsic" motivation, can be confusing here. A person is intrinsically motivated when he or she engages in an activity "for its own sake" and extrinsically motivated when engaging in an activity for the sake of something unconnected to the activity itself. Intrinsic motivators are entirely internal—curiosity is probably the best example—and people with high levels of intrinsic motivation are what we call self-motivated. "Extrinsic motivators" are external, such as praise, rewards, and what I have called incentives "strictly speaking."[98] But all "extrinsic motivators" are not alike. Praise and rewards do not operate in the same way as incentives. Incentives are tangible benefits unrelated to the activity itself. For example, giving a student candy for reading a book is an incentive. Telling the child that you are proud of him for reading the book or allowing him a special opportunity to tell the class about the book is not an incentive. These latter approaches reinforce the value of the activity and may enhance intrinsic motivation by increasing the child's desire to undertake the activity "for its own sake." Incentives, because their value is unrelated to the value of the learning, can have the opposite effect. I am concerned here only with evaluating the use of incentives strictly speaking in motivating children to learn, and "pay for grades" programs clearly qualify as incentives in this sense.

Behavioral psychologists, as we saw in chapter 2, focus exclusively on extrinsic motivators, discounting intrinsic motivation altogether. Everything is learned by the organism as it responds to its environment. People, like other organisms, are passive and malleable. Because all motivation is extrinsic, anyone who can control environmental stimuli can control the organism. This was the theoretical perspective that first led to "token economies," beginning with chimpanzees in the 1930s and then with mental patients, prisoners, and schoolchildren. Patients in mental hospitals, for example, could earn tokens for compliant behavior that they could then trade in for personal items in the hospital store. Token economies are very similar to "pay for grades" schemes, and the controversies they provoked are almost indistinguishable from the controversies today.[99]

Contemporary defenders of incentives in schools argue that they work when all else fails. They consider their opponents to be idealists who are caught up in a fantasy of pure motivation.[100] Drawing on the behaviorist view that there is no intrinsic motivation, they see no appreciable difference between working for money, for grades, for praise, or for the glory that comes with winning a competition. In other words, extrinsic motivators of one form or another are the only tool we have to motivate children to learn. Young children in particular respond well to short-term motivators. Even if some people do put effort into learning without constant reinforcement, such behavior requires a level of maturity that most children simply do not have.

Critics dispute the contention that incentives work reliably and add the claim that their impact on character and values is primarily negative. In a wide variety of situations, recent research in economics has shown that incentives can backfire.[101] British women offered cash to donate blood are almost 50 percent *less* likely to give blood than women who are asked and offered nothing.[102] Swiss citizens are significantly *less* likely to accept siting a nuclear waste facility in their area if monetary compensation is offered as an inducement.[103] Indian research subjects offered large bonuses to complete simple tasks performed *less* well than subjects given smaller bonuses.[104] American shoppers, urged to buy a particular kind of bread, were *less* willing to buy that kind when given a small additional cash incentive.[105]

There is a vast literature in psychology showing similar results of the effects of incentives on learning. If children are interested in a task, solving puzzles, for example, and you tell them that they will be rewarded for completing some puzzles, they perform less well and lose interest sooner than children who are not rewarded or expecting a reward. The incentive, or extrinsic motivation, diminishes the intrinsic motivation. It turns play into work, decreasing both enthusiasm for the task and the level of performance. In this way, incentives can be counterproductive with respect to learning.[106]

What we know from decades of research in this area is that incentives can work to increase performance with intrinsically boring, routine tasks and to increase behavioral compliance. But these gains are only temporary: when the incentive is removed, the subject reverts to the original performance level or behavior. Incentives are positively counterproductive when the learning task requires creativity or problem-solving skills. Extrinsic motivators of all kinds work best when the classroom environment is supportive and when they are used to impart information (e.g., as a sign that you did a good job), which can contribute to a sense of competence. When they are perceived as a controlling mechanism, they decrease intrinsic motivation—and intrinsic motivation is strongly associated with higher achievement overall.[107]

Moreover, incentives undermine altruism, reciprocity, and other non-self-interested motives in a manner similar to the way in which they undermine intrinsic motivation. Think of the blood donors and the nuclear waste site experiment mentioned above. The evidence suggests that when ethical motives and self-interested motives are both present, they do not act independently or reinforce each other. Instead, introducing self-interested incentives has negative effects, "crowding out" ethical motives while failing in themselves to produce the desired behavior.[108] This implies, for example, that using incentives to encourage student participation in a community service program would be counterproductive, whereas a community service requirement might succeed, delivering the message that giving to others is a responsibility everyone is expected to fulfill.

In addition to "crowding out," incentives can have a "spillover effect." If you pay your child to mow the lawn, he or she is less likely to willingly do the dishes for free. Relying on incentives in one area can affect attitudes and behavior in other areas.[109] By introducing payment in a family setting, you introduce the norms of the commercial domain, or the market, into a realm previously governed by different, more cooperative norms of family or community responsibility.

One way to think of the issue is to ask yourself whether a school should be more like a factory or more like a family in its governing norms. A school is designed to serve the needs of its students, and the students' learning ought to benefit them directly. In a factory, on the other hand, workers produce for the benefit of the company, receive no direct benefit from their work, and are therefore compensated for their efforts. Introducing monetary incentives into the school setting can corrode the institutional culture over the long run and impact areas not directly related to the incentive program itself.*

Monetary incentives are based on the premise that people are motivated by self-interest. The problem is that operating on the basis of that premise becomes a self-fulfilling prophecy. (One study shows that taking an economics class that teaches that people are self-interested increases students' selfish behavior.)[110]

---

*This also applies to the use of incentives to motivate teachers.

In an educational setting, if monetary incentives are employed, students learn that the only question it is important to ask is, "What's in this for me?" And, not surprisingly, this leads to an increase in cheating as well.

This is a general result of the use of incentives. Where people are paid to give blood, more of them will lie about their health status.[111] Where teachers' incentives are tied to students' test performance, more teachers will change their students' answers on the exam sheets.[112] Where students work in an environment that values only extrinsic rewards for learning, cheating goes up.[113]

Alasdair MacIntyre illustrates the point with the example of a seven-year-old child enticed to play chess by the promise of candy if he plays and more candy if he wins. So long as the child is motivated by the candy, he has every reason to cheat and no reason not to cheat. But when the child comes to be motivated by the desire to master the game and to excel at it, if he cheats to win, he will be defeating only himself. The candy is a good external to the practice of playing chess. The mastery of certain skills is a good internal to that practice.[114]

Contemporary studies of the effectiveness of new "pay for grades" incentive programs tend to track the findings of decades of research in psychology: incentives have negative results in some circumstances and positive results in others. Most studies show little or no impact on achievement or learning, but some show that incentives have positive effects on attendance.[115] In some of the studies, payments increase performance. But the researchers remark that the gains result not from the money itself but from the fact that the incentives confirm the students' perception of themselves as high achievers.[116] Few studies look at long-term results.[117] None attempts to test changes in attitudes as well as changes in test scores or grades; the question of character is simply not addressed. And none attempts to correct for cheating to be sure that observed improvements are real. For these reasons, the studies are unlikely to settle this controversy once and for all.[118]

When I said that this is a very old debate, I had in mind John

Locke's letters on education first published in 1693.[119] They contain very clear statements of the basic arguments behind the critique of incentives to motivate learning. First, there *is* such a thing as intrinsic motivation, and education should take advantage of that by allowing children to learn through play. Locke recommends alphabet dice for spelling games. Moreover, children, like everyone else, resent constraint. Being told that you must do something will diminish your desire to do it. Second, education aims at cultivating virtue (character), and virtue requires the ability to resist desires and follow where reason leads instead. This is why rewards and punishments (incentives), especially corporal punishment, are so counterproductive with children. They teach them only to consider a kind of calculus of pains and pleasures—to ask themselves whether the pleasure of the transgression is worth the expected punishment or whether the effort of the task is worth the pleasure of the expected reward.

Incentives *cannot* teach self-discipline. This is a crucial point: incentives are worse than useless if character is your primary concern. Locke recommends praise and blame, esteem and disgrace instead. These are not subject to calculation in the same way as reward and punishment. The child does not ask herself, "How can I get the most of what I want with the least effort?" Instead, the child seeks to earn the respect and approval of her parents.* In this way, she comes to internalize their standards and develop self-discipline and a sense of responsibility. Lastly, respect for the child is a critical component of successful educational practice.

In education as in any other sphere, incentives are a tool with inherent limitations. Precisely because they are extrinsic motivators, they are a short-term fix. Once they are removed, their effectiveness ends. Incentives treat symptoms and not causes; they are a superficial fix. Since they do not address causes, they

---

*Adults, according to Locke, need to develop some independence from the concern for reputation and the approval of others. But children are appropriately governed by the standards of the adults around them.

will be needed indefinitely if nothing else is done. And incentives raise issues of fairness: are payments for grades fair to the child who makes a huge effort but cannot raise her grade? And since we know that extrinsic rewards can be counterproductive for those who are already motivated, is a "pay for grades" program fair to them?

Despite all of the force of the critics' arguments, I do believe that it is sometimes legitimate to use incentives to motivate learning. But they need to be employed in ways that reflect what we already know. For example, we know that they will work better for learning spelling, multiplication tables, and other routine tasks than for reading comprehension or problem solving.

Yes, incentives undermine intrinsic motivation—but in some circumstances, students may have little intrinsic motivation to begin with. In such circumstances, a child might try something, on account of the temptation of an incentive, that he or she has been afraid to try or has been uninterested in trying. Having discovered that success is possible, the child may no longer need the incentive. The incentive would work like a "jump start" for a dead battery.

But then the car needs to keep running on its own. We need to think about how to transition from incentives to self-motivation or to sustained habits. We know that incentives only work in the short term. Therefore, incentive programs ought to be designed with the goal of making the incentive obsolete, including specific steps to meet that goal. The problem, of course, is that incentive programs create the conditions for their own perpetuation by encouraging students to work only when rewarded. This is the paradoxical situation they can create.

The legitimacy of incentives to motivate learning also depends a great deal on the type of incentive employed. Contrast cash payment with a quite different extrinsic motivator. My children had a kindergarten teacher who made a "bookworm" for each child that "grew" by one link each time the child completed reading a book.[120] I am sure that the children were motivated by the pleasure of watching their bookworm "grow" as well as by the pleasure of reading a book.* But the bookworm had no meaning other than as a sign of their accomplishment and of the value of their learning.

The legitimacy of incentives depends on their meaning and context. One author distinguishes "if-then" motivators from "now-that" motivators. The first are conditional and set up expectations before the task is attempted; if you do something for me, then will I do something for you. The latter acknowledge a job well done after the task is completed: now that you have done something well, I will acknowledge and reward your achievement.[121] Recall that incentives differ from rewards and communicate different things.[122] It is the second, rewards, that are much more likely to be effective with students. A comparable situation arises in employment. When employers "incentivize" each task, using incentives excessively, they send a message also: they communicate that they distrust their employees. In these cases, the incentives are not likely to increase productivity.[123]

What does a "pay for grades" program communicate? It implies that the activity is not worth doing for its own sake. It communicates materialistic values—only money and the things that money can buy count in life.[124] And it may communicate low expectations of the students, saying to them: you cannot be expected to act responsibly without payoffs. For this reason, some critics of these programs view them as condescending.

If you attend to the meaning of the incentive, the difference becomes apparent between cash payments and a college scholarship, for example, even though some researchers put both kinds of programs into the same category.[125] The college scholarship is a little bit like the bookworm. It is a sign of achievement that reinforces the idea that education is what is truly valuable. College scholarships are monetary incentives, but they are far preferable

---

*People always have mixed motivations. The question of whether people are *only* motivated extrinsically or should *only* be motivated intrinsically is a red herring.

to cash payments for just this reason. The benefit the student receives is not so much the money as it is further education.

Finally, context matters. "Pay for grades" programs are a sign of the failure of an educational system. Providing incentives for incentives is a kind of last-ditch effort. Are these incentive programs a good thing? Is putting a cast on your leg a good thing? Only if it is broken—otherwise, the cast would be damaging, weakening the leg.

Thus, although incentives would never be my educational tool of choice, and cash payments would be among the least preferred type of incentive, even cash payments might be the recommended treatment in some circumstances. Payments for attendance, for example, may actually work to get students to school; a good attendance record is within everyone's reach, and you can't teach students who aren't there.

Context matters in a different sense as well. All kinds of extrinsic motivators, incentives included, work best when they are administered in an atmosphere of support and respect. And contrariwise, incentives that are experienced as controlling or insulting backfire. In explaining the surprising fact that incentives often undermine performance, all of the researchers, both economists and psychologists, emphasize this aspect of incentives. They speak of the importance of an individual's sense of autonomy or self-determination.[126] People react negatively when they feel that their freedom of action is threatened. And contrariwise, the more an individual is treated as a responsible agent and the less he or she is made to feel like a puppet, the more effective the incentive will be.

This is why the frequency of the use of incentives in schooling is also an important consideration. They are most likely to be effective if used sparingly. If they are the dominant mode of relating to children, they create a counterproductive controlling environment. This observation leads one step further. Since incentives are a form of power that necessarily has an element of control, we would do well to focus our attention on alternative means of inspiring effort and motivating learning.

The controversy over incentives to motivate learning can be characterized as a contest between "Mandevillians" and "moralists." In this case, the Mandevillians are the behaviorists who are enthusiastic about all kinds of incentives in education because they focus on academic outcomes with little regard for character development. The moralists, the harshest critics of incentives, focus on character and seem to imagine the possibility of pure motivation for learning. But these extremes miss the central point. Character development and learning cannot be separated. They are the twin purposes of education. And when it comes to learning, character and outcomes are inextricably linked. The way students are motivated has a direct effect on their effort and performance. Why we do things impacts how well we do them.

Incentive programs ought to come with a "caution" label. They have been shown repeatedly to undermine motivation and performance, as well as to corrode character. We have seen them backfire. Moreover, there are inherent limits to their usefulness over the long term. Nonetheless, all incentives are not alike and circumstances differ. It would be foolish to condemn their use altogether. Incentives can be used to enhance performance on routine tasks and to increase behavioral compliance in the short run. They should be used sparingly in an otherwise noncontrolling environment and with careful attention to meaning and context. Incentives ought to be thoughtfully employed, in full awareness of what we already know about what they can and cannot do.[127]

Chapter SEVEN

BEYOND VOLUNTARINESS

As we have seen, examining the particulars of incentive programs in some detail in order to evaluate their legitimacy raises a host of complex questions. Often, however, discussions of the ethics of incentives hang the question solely on whether the response to the offer is voluntary. But voluntariness alone is inadequate as a standard for judging the complex issues involved in most cases. Where does the focus on voluntariness come from, and what are its limits?

A major source of the emphasis on "voluntariness" comes from the approach to incentives in contemporary economics. Incentives are considered trades and trades are considered ethical. Trades are both voluntary and mutually beneficial. Both parties agree to the exchange voluntarily only because they believe that they will be better off as a result. There appear to be two standards at work here: voluntariness and benefit. But since, in this view, there is no objective standard of benefit, my choice becomes the sole test of what counts as beneficial. Because no distinction is made between my preferences and what is actually good for me or the right thing for me to do, the two standards collapse into one. Consequently, the only real ethical question regarding any exchange, incentives included, is whether it is voluntary. Voluntary consent becomes the sole criterion for judging the legitimacy of an incentive.

The result is that other sorts of ethical concerns are either neglected or squeezed into the vocabulary of coercion and consent in a distorted form. This problem appeared in the discussion of recruiting research subjects, in the discussion of plea bargaining, and, to a lesser extent, in the discussion of IMF loan conditionality. But it also appears in many other areas, such as markets for organs or surrogate motherhood, where ethical concerns about monetary incentives are often framed as concerns about voluntariness. We tend to focus on the question of whether these offers are "irresistible," "excessive," and hence "coercive," constituting "undue inducement," particularly when the incentives are large and the target population is poor. But, surely, there is nothing wrong in itself with offering money to people who need it most. As we have seen, the real ethical issue here is not the size of an "excessive" offer that seems to compromise free choice. Behind the issue of "undue inducements" is the concern that people are being asked to do something about which they may have serious misgivings or about which they ought to have serious misgivings.

To offer another example, in the case of plea bargaining, the question arose about the ethics of offering leniency with a large sentence differential to a defendant when the evidence against him is weak. The debate centers on whether these offers are "coercive" and whether the defendant acts under duress. The defendant is certainly under pressure when the cost of refusing the offer seems "prohibitive." But quite apart from what is going on inside the mind of the defendant when he makes his choice, there is the question of the prosecutor's duty. *Should* a prosecutor seek a guilty plea when he believes there is insufficient evidence to convict in open court? The question ought to be asked, at least. To approach incentives as a form of trade narrows the ethical inquiry to the question of voluntariness and makes it more difficult to recognize other sorts of ethical issues on their own terms, particularly issues about the responsibilities of those in positions of power.

Reinforcing our emphasis on "voluntariness" as the ethical measure of incentives is another tendency—a general reluctance to make substantive moral judgments about other people's choices. As long as everyone involved is a consenting adult, who are we to judge? This attitude may rest on a laudable concern to avoid paternalism in all of its forms, but it also radically narrows the conversation. At a recent convention of psychologists and social workers, the suggestion was made that sadomasochism be deleted from the list of pathologies, and the proposal was discussed among participants. Those opposed argued that such behavior is compulsive and hence cannot be considered voluntary—*as if consent were the only issue.*[1] One might expect the conversation to include discussion of what it means for people to take pleasure in cruelty and suffering and whether such people do or do not need help.

My aim is to take the conversation beyond voluntariness to encompass the complete array of ethical issues that arise when considering the ethics of incentives. Voluntariness is surely a necessary condition for the legitimacy of an incentive, but it is not a sufficient condition. With voluntariness as the only standard, there is no argument to condemn exploitation, undue influence, or bribery, for example.[2] Suppose a person bribes a judge to allow a guilty person to go free. Both the one offering the bribe and the judge voluntarily participate in the exchange and both benefit. The judge chooses freely between accepting additional cash and carrying out his responsibilities. But clearly these two options are not alike. And the ethical assessment of the transaction depends on our ability to distinguish between them.

There are many kinds of bargains or exchanges, all voluntary, but not all equally ethical or legitimate. Consider the array of possibilities in legislative bargaining. Legislators could buy and sell their votes to the highest bidder, considering only their own self-interest. They could swap votes, agreeing to vote for each other's favorite projects, in order to secure a majority for legislation that may or may not serve the public interest. Or they could negotiate a compromise that serves the public interest by helping form a majority where each side relinquishes some of what it wants so long as the other side does the same. The ethical differences between these types of bargains are obvious where considerations of purpose and character are in play. Yet, these three types of bargains would look quite similar if they were considered simply as trades—voluntary and mutually beneficial transactions.[3]

A very different sort of experience illustrates the same point. Consider a three-year-old child, afraid to sleep in his own room, wanting to sleep in his parents' bed. The parents know that they will get no sleep if they allow the child to join them. Let us rule out coercion (locking the child's door until morning) and persuasion (telling the child that there is nothing to be afraid of—true, and a good thing to say, but likely to be totally ineffective). This leaves bargaining, of which at least two types are possible. In the first case, the parents offer to buy the child a highly desirable toy if the child stays in his own room. In the second case, the parents offer to allow the child to bring a pillow and blanket into their room and sleep on the floor beside their bed. In both cases, everyone will go to sleep (if they are lucky), and that legitimate aim is met. In both cases, the parents present the child with a choice.

Nonetheless, the two sorts of negotiations are quite different in their consequences for "character." The first is an incentive, whereas the second is more like a negotiated agreement where common ground is found after both parties yield something of their ideal position. The lesson of the first for the child is that those with resources (the parents) can legitimately use them to set the terms of a situation to get what they want (although, like some other incentive offers, it may backfire—suppose the child says, "I'd rather sleep in your bed than have the toy"). In contrast, the lesson of the second is that mutual accommodation is possible. The parents set a limit that the child must accept—he can't sleep in their bed. But then, there is a search for a compromise. Moreover, in the first case, the child still goes to bed frightened. In the second, his anxiety is addressed. In fact, the purpose of the negotiation might be said to be not only a good night's sleep for everyone but assisting the child in learning to manage anxiety, which is part of a parent's responsibility. The point is that the two bargains would look quite similar if they were considered simply as trades—voluntary and mutually beneficial transactions. The very real differences between them only appear when questions about purpose and character are raised. And indeed, these are just the sorts of questions concerned parents worry about.

The thrust of my argument is that voluntariness is not the sole criterion for judging incentives, just as it is not the sole criterion for judging other sorts of power; legitimacy of purpose and effects on character are also basic standards. But there is a second problem with the conception of voluntariness as an ethical criterion.

Voluntariness itself can be understood in different ways. Minimally construed, voluntariness means only "to have a choice." But rats in a maze have lots of choices—left or right, left or right, left or right. This is not the kind of choice that has ethical value. We value voluntariness, as an ethical criterion, to the extent that it is an expression of freedom. But what we might call "mere" voluntariness is not always an expression of freedom. Let us consider "truly voluntary" action to be autonomous action.

"To have a choice" is not the same thing as "to act autonomously." Isaiah Berlin's depiction of "positive freedom" captures the elements of what I mean by "autonomy" as well as the connections between freedom, rationality, and moral responsibility. It is worth quoting at length.

> The "positive" sense of the word "liberty" derives from the wish on the part of the individual to be his own master.... I wish my life and decisions to depend on myself, not on

external forces of whatever kind . . . I wish to be somebody, not nobody; a doer—deciding, not being decided for, self-directed and not acted upon by external nature or by other men as if I were a thing, or an animal, or a slave incapable of playing a human role, that is, of conceiving goals and policies of my own and realizing them. This is at least a part of what I mean when I say that I am rational, and that it is my reason that distinguishes me as a human being from the rest of the world. *I wish, above all, to be conscious of myself as a thinking, willing, active being, bearing responsibility for my choices and able to explain them by references to my own ideas and purposes.*[4]

In chapter 4, we saw that the standards for legitimate use of power presupposed an understanding of human beings as free and rational agents capable of moral responsibility. This understanding leads me to suggest an alternative to the minimal construction of voluntariness. This alternative, more robust sense of voluntariness would move beyond voluntariness as "mere" choice toward voluntariness as autonomy.

For the sake of clarity, allow me to exaggerate the contrasts in what I will call the two conceptions of voluntariness: Voluntariness I (choice) and Voluntariness II (autonomy). These two conceptions have very different implications for the evaluation of incentives. Voluntariness I is a standard that can be met so long as the incentive is not coercive. Voluntariness II is a more demanding requirement that leads to considering—and criticizing—manipulative, exploitive, paternalistic, and seductive offers as well.

On the basis of Voluntariness I, we would expect incentives to be effective whenever they offer a person an attractive choice. Voluntariness II, on the other hand, provides a basis for understanding why incentives sometimes backfire. Simply put, they backfire when they are experienced as a threat to autonomy. In general, people react negatively when their autonomy is threatened, and sometimes those reactions seem irrational. People will reject offers of advice just because they want to decide for themselves.[5] People will become irritated when a person offers a favor because the favor might entail a reciprocal obligation, and so forth.

Something similar happens in the case of incentives as well, as we saw in the discussion of the use of incentives to motivate students. The incentive, which is an extrinsic motivator, conflicts with intrinsic motivation. Intrinsic motivation is a form of autonomy: self-directed behavior, not depending on external forces. When extrinsic and intrinsic motivation conflict, or when incentives conflict with autonomous action and judgment, either the intrinsic motivation and autonomy are "crowded out" or the incentive is rejected and backfires.[6]

In other words, incentives can be insulting. People like to think of themselves as free and rational and to be treated accordingly. Incentives, especially when they attempt to micromanage behavior, can communicate distrust of your motives, particularly ethical motives, and disrespect for your ability to make an independent judgment. If this is what is communicated, the incentives will provoke resentment and will not work as expected.

Incentive programs that treat people with respect not only pass the highest ethical test, they also produce the best outcomes. And where incentives are experienced as disrespectful in some way, alternative approaches that take "the respect factor" into account work better. Again, examples range across a variety of domains. Early College Schools allow minority high school students to earn college credit at no cost during their senior year in high school. Participants in this program are a representative sample of students from low-performing schools. For these students, the dropout rate plummeted and academic achievement improved. One administrator attributes the success of the program to "what high expectations can do."[7] A new series of successful programs to reduce crime and improve compliance with parole conditions relies not on severe sanctions but on increasing the perceived legitimacy of the system. People are much more likely to obey rules that they perceive to be fair: "All these strategies are a way of signaling to groups of people that government agents view them with dignity, neutrality and trust which convinces them that government has a right to hold them accountable."[8] The proponents of a new approach to economics, called identity economics, argue that in well-run organizations, employees identify with the organization. Such organizations cultivate a sense of responsibility on the part of employees, and employees perform better. In contrast, performance pay and bonuses demonstrate bad faith, telling employees that they are not trusted to do the right thing.[9] Finally, if the problem is tax compliance, you might think that greater likelihood of detection of tax avoidance and stiffer fines would be the solution. But in one Swiss study, this approach had no systematic success. On the other hand, there was considerable evidence in studies of several different countries that tax compliance is lower where citizens have fewer opportunities for participation and higher where citizens have greater opportunities for participation. When citizens are trusted to act independently, they also develop greater trust in the legitimacy of the system and are more likely to comply with its demands.[10]

Of course, incentives are not always insulting and they do not always backfire. When an airline offers an incentive in the form of a gift to induce you to choose to ride their planes, the problem does not arise at all. The choice of which plane to take is always based on a mix of various external factors. When a drug company offers physicians a gift to induce them to prescribe their medicines, the situation is quite different. The choice of which medicines to prescribe is understood as a matter of professional judgment to be decided on the merits. Autonomy is at stake here—including "bearing responsibility for my choices and [being] able to explain them." In the first case, it is perfectly fine to explain your choice of airline with the statement "because I got a free trip to Hawaii." For the doctor to explain to a patient that she is prescribing a certain medication "because I got a free trip to Hawaii" is really not acceptable. A doctor with some professional pride might well experience a gross attempt to influence her judgment as an insult.

Or, I should say, she ought to experience it as an insult. People ought to be prickly about their autonomy, especially in a democracy (a point to which I shall return in the next chapter). But people can get used to an "incentivized" environment. They become desensitized, and the assumption of incentives—that people are primarily moved by calculations of extrinsic benefits and costs—becomes self-fulfilling. This is what it means to say that incentives can corrode institutional culture.

The possibility of a conflict between Voluntariness I and Voluntariness II has been recognized by others as well, though using different language. Two psychologists, Edward Deci and Richard Ryan, write about the problem in the context of motivating learning. Incentives, especially when they create a controlling environment in the classroom, diminish intrinsic motivation. And the development of intrinsic motivation is crucial for the sense of competence, autonomy, and relatedness, which are the key components of self-determination.[11] Similarly, the economist Bruno Frey argues that in order to understand the effects of incentives, we need a richer psychology. He suggests replacing *homo oeconomicus*, the economic man who chooses on the basis of extrinsic factors, with *homo oeconomicus maturus*, a new model incorporating intrinsic motivation as well.[12] Ernst Fehr and Armin Falk, also economists, have shown that we cannot understand how incentives really work unless we recognize that important human motivations include reciprocity, social approval, and the desire to do interesting work.[13]

I, too, am concerned to move beyond the limited psychology presupposed by Voluntariness I. Whether rooted in the psychology of behaviorism (behavior as the organism's response to environmental stimuli) or in the psychological presuppositions of rational choice economics (behavior as the interaction of preferences and external constraints),[14] Voluntariness I flattens the ethical landscape. In this view, incentives offer people choices and they respond freely. Moreover, they also respond predictably. If you understand people's preferences and can control their environment, you can steer them in the direction you want them to go. People are passive and malleable, and their behavior is not fundamentally different from that of the rat in the maze. For these reasons, they can be successfully subjected to social engineering with incentives as the primary tool.

The historical origins of incentives, discussed in chapter 2, show their close connection to both behavioral psychology and social engineering. These connections seem unproblematic from the perspective of Voluntariness I. But once the claims of Voluntariness II are considered, a paradox appears at the heart of the problem of the ethics of incentives. Incentives that allow for choice may nonetheless undermine autonomy. Incentives are lauded as the preferred tool of public policy precisely because they enhance freedom by preserving choice. At the same time, their success as instruments of social engineering or social control depends on people reacting to them in predictable ways. They invite the sort of choice that is a self-interested calculation of benefit. They tend to inhibit autonomous action, deliberation over purposes, ethical judgment, or self-direction. Paradoxically, incentives are at once freedom-enhancing and a threat to freedom. To appreciate this paradox requires moving beyond voluntariness to recognize that the real issues are the meaning of freedom and the use and abuse of power.

Chapter EIGHT
A Different Kind of Conversation

Incentives are an attractive tool for public policy and private management for two basic reasons. First, they seem to enhance freedom because they preserve choice and are an alternative to coercion. Second, they offer the promise of an easy solution, a "quick fix": if you can get the price right, an incentive ought to produce predictable changes in behavior immediately.

But incentives are deceptive. We have seen that there are many situations in which incentives do not produce predictable results—quite the contrary. Incentives can be counterproductive; sometimes they backfire. Moreover, attaching strings does not always make the puppet dance, as we saw in the case of IMF loan conditions. And incentives, because they generally do not address the root causes of the problem, are often limited as a tool for long-term improvements. Political problems are not always reducible to engineering problems.

Incentives are also deceptive because, when governors and managers employ incentives, they are attempting to steer people's choices in certain directions. But because incentives do leave people with a choice, managers remain in a position to deny the extent of their own control and to evade accountability. This is another aspect of incentives that makes them an attractive tool from a manager's point of view. They are an exercise of power that conceals power.

Finally, incentives are deceptive to the extent that they conflate choice and freedom. Having choices is not the whole story when it comes to freedom. Authorities from various institutions try to direct people's behavior in all kinds of ways, while leaving them with plenty of choices. This book began with a list of contemporary incentives, all designed to direct people's behavior: to eat in a certain way, stay married, practice religion, read particular books, and have fewer children—all without commands, all without any obvious infringement of freedom. But imagine a world where incentives were employed in every domain to direct every kind of behavior—such a world would seem Orwellian indeed.

Incentives have a kind of paradoxical or double-sided quality, seeming to both preserve and compromise freedom. This is part of what makes the question of the ethics of incentives both fascinating and difficult. But the dominant contemporary conversation about incentives completely obscures their complexity. Incentives today are simply identified with voluntary exchange and assumed to be inherently ethical. In stark contrast, the conversation about incentives at the turn of the twentieth century in America is particularly revealing of the complexities of the issues. Then, incentives were viewed not as an alternative to social engineering but as a tool of social engineering. They were viewed as a form of power, just as problematic ethically and politically as any of its other forms.

Adopting this insight, I have tried to shift the terms of the conversation in a number of ways:

- From "trade" to "power." Incentives are both. To recognize only the former is a mistake.

- From power understood as a simple ethical continuum (coercion-bargaining-persuasion) to power understood in all its complexity—with coercion, bargaining, and persuasion each occurring in legitimate and illegitimate forms. One must ask what *kind* of bargain any given incentive is in order to judge it.
- From voluntariness as the only ethical standard to purpose, character, voluntariness, effectiveness, equity, and undue influence all being relevant standards. Every one of these considerations matters for assessing the use and abuse of power.
- From limited voluntariness to maximum autonomy—replacing mere choice and rational calculation with a more robust conception of freedom and rationality. The best uses of power respect human beings as active agents capable of moral responsibility.
- From a focus on the offeree to a focus on the offerer. Some offers should not be made even if the individual can freely refuse them. The question is not only one of the individual psychology of the person offered an incentive but also of the responsibilities of those making the offer—the powerful—both in public and in private life.

One of our most common conversations today is the one that circles around the question of whether a particular problem should be handled by government or by markets. But incentives are a tool of both public and private power. We have a tendency to obscure that fact because we identify incentives with market mechanisms. Defenders of market solutions assume that governments, employing coercive regulations, stand in contrast to markets, which employ voluntary incentives. And because incentives are trades that are voluntary, it is assumed that the "mutually beneficial," and hence ethical, solutions of the marketplace are to be preferred.[1] Like the "moralists" versus the "Mandevillians," this is an "all or nothing" framing of the problem.

135

I am suggesting an alternative conceptual framework that allows us to distinguish legitimate from illegitimate incentives whether we find them in public or private arenas. The distinction between public and private, or government and markets, is often less important than the distinction between legitimate and illegitimate incentives. To make that distinction requires considering under what conditions the incentive is being offered, by whom, to whom, and for what reason. It also requires considering not only whether or not the incentive allows for choice but also whether or not it respects autonomy.

All of this suggests that there are important questions about incentives beyond the problem of judging the legitimacy of any single incentive in any particular case. What are the political implications for a democratic society where incentives are the preferred tool of policy and management and where incentives have become both ubiquitous and uncontroversial?

Incentives presuppose that people are reactive and motivated by calculations of self-interest, and of course, very often they are. Moreover, we have seen that incentives themselves can make that presupposition a self-fulfilling prophecy. The more we accept incentives in different areas of life, the more acceptable they seem. People can become more passive, self-interested, predictable, and manipulable.

This image stands in contrast to a certain kind of democratic ideal—an ideal of government by the people—that presupposes citizens who are active, autonomous agents, capable of developing and pursuing their own life projects.[2] Such citizens are also capable of acting on the basis of "noncalculative" motives[3] and of engaging in deliberation with others to reach judgments on the merits of the issues before them. In highly incentivized environments, are these the sorts of capacities that will flourish? I think not. And that is a real problem. The sense of insult that incentives can provoke is worth cultivating. It reflects the impulse to protect one's autonomy, and as such, it is an important support for democratic politics. Thus the ethical question of "effect on character" turns out to be a critical *political* question as well.[4]

Incentives may also inhibit deliberation and judgment directly. They can circumvent the need for persuasion by giving people extrinsic reasons for the choices they make. Consider these contrasting depictions of how two organizations, both believing themselves to be "non-authoritarian," might go about instituting a new policy. One organization informs its members of various policy changes under consideration and seeks their feedback and suggestions. People are given opportunities to discuss the proposals among themselves. Once a decision is made, after the alternatives have had a fair hearing, the members are again informed of the decision and of the reasons for it. At the end of this process, the members are expected to comply with the new policy. The new policy may not be their preferred alternative or the best one possible, but everyone will have been part of the discussion and everyone will have heard the case to be made for it.

Another organization adopts a new policy after a decision at the highest levels[5] and offers incentives to those in the organization to change their behavior so as to be in line with the new policy. Each individual then makes an independent decision as to whether to change his or her behavior for the sake of the benefit being offered. But nobody need understand the reasons for the new policy or its meaning for the organization as a whole in order to reach that decision. And there is no reason for consideration of the new policy on the merits or for discussion among the organization's members.

There are two points to be made here. First, although the members of the second organization have a choice, it is not obvious that they have greater freedom in any meaningful sense than those in the first organization who participate in the process. Second, the use of incentives in the second organization is a substitute for persuasion. While we readily recognize that incentives are an alternative to coercion, we rarely see the way in which they substitute for persuasion. And persuasion is crucial for democracy. A democratic society requires processes of persuasion and deliberation throughout its social institutions.

This is one reason to be critical of social engineering; it tends to inhibit processes of persuasion. One of our current political conversations pits proponents of social engineering and opponents of government intervention, libertarians in particular, against one another. But it is perfectly possible to criticize social engineering without seeing all government action as negative and without adopting a libertarian point of view, which makes individual choice the dominant value. Once again, I seek to alter the conversation. What many social engineers and many libertarians *share* is a set of assumptions about human psychology and behavior often encapsulated in the phrase "*homo oeconomicus.*"[6] This is the economic man who seeks to benefit himself and who guides his behavior by calculating the balance of costs and benefits involved in any course of action, always responding to the incentives in his environment. With this psychological starting point, social engineers and libertarians alike will tend to find incentives generally benign and will tend to reach for a new incentive system in response to each new problem.

But from an alternative psychological perspective, the general trend toward the increased use of incentives in public and private life is highly problematic. It raises the questions "What kind of citizens are we likely to produce?" and "What kind of citizens do we aspire to be?" These issues appear when we consider not *homo oeconomicus* but a different sort of person: one who has complex motivations (some intrinsic and others extrinsic), one who has multiple purposes and has actively shaped them, one who tries to fulfill her responsibilities as well as furthering her interests. With this sort of person in mind, we can approach particular proposed incentives with some discrimination. This is the argument put forward by Samuel Bowles in his recent work, where he shows that incentives undermine the very virtues necessary to sustain markets, for example, honesty, the work ethic, and promise-keeping.[7] He concludes that we need to employ incentives in sophisticated ways that take into account what we know about the conditions under which they "backfire" or "crowd out" virtue.

A discriminating use of incentives would go a long way toward addressing the problem. But I question whether better, smarter incentives can be the whole solution. Bowles himself points out that one of the reasons incentives fail is that they conflict with people's desires for autonomy, for self-determination, and to be respected as a member of a community—the very desires associated with democratic virtues. This suggests that incentives should not be the only tool in the policymaker's toolbox. Policymakers need to find alternative approaches—alternatives based on a broader view of human motivation and designed to enhance the qualities of autonomy and agency necessary for active democratic citizenship.

During the Progressive era in America, there was an animated debate over the democratic ideal of popular government.[8] Are the people capable of self-government? If not, could democracy be improved by empowering experts? Is self-government a primary good, an essential element of human dignity and self-realization, or is democracy justified by its ability to provide people with a decent living, health, security, and so forth? Can social engineering be a force for democratic improvement, or does it undermine democracy by treating citizens like puppets on a string? It is not accidental that these issues were at the center of the conversation during the time that incentives first appeared on the scene. It would be a very good thing to revitalize that conversation and to struggle with those questions once again.

Notes

Preface

1. Sophocles, *Philoctetes*, in *Sophocles II: Ajax, The Women of Trachis, Electra & Philoctetes*, ed. David Grene and Richard Lattimore (Chicago: University of Chicago Press, 1969), scene 1, lines 88–90.

Chapter One
Why Worry about Incentives?

1. Hans Jonas, "Philosophical Reflections on Experimenting with Human Subjects," *Daedalus* 98, no. 2 (1969): 219–47.

2. Kenneth Arrow, "Gifts and Exchanges," *Philosophy and Public Affairs* 1, no. 4 (1972): 343–62; Peter Singer, "Altruism and Commerce: A Defense of Titmuss against Arrow," *Philosophy and Public Affairs* 2, no. 3 (1973): 312–20; Richard Titmuss, *The Gift Relationship* (New York: The New Press, 1997).

3. Richard H. Thaler and Cass R. Sunstein, *Nudge: Improving Decisions about Health, Wealth, and Happiness* (New Haven: Yale University Press, 2008).

4. Additional ethical issues may arise over "externalities," i.e., the impact of the transaction on third parties. See, for example, G. A. Cohen, "Robert Nozick and Wilt Chamberlain: How Patterns Preserve Liberty," *Erkenntnis* 11 (1977): 5–23; Michael J. Trebilcock, *The Limits of Freedom of Contract* (Cambridge, MA: Harvard University Press, 1993), chap. 3.

5. Some identify persuasion entirely with rational conviction, which does not compromise free choice, and hence do not view persuasion as a form of power. See, for example, Jürgen Habermas, *Moral Consciousness and Communicative Action*, trans. Christian Lenhardt and Shierry Weber (Cambridge, MA: MIT Press, 1990), 88–99. But persuasion often involves irrational mental processes as well. See Robert B. Cialdini, *Influence: Science and Practice*, 5th ed. (Boston: Pearson, 2009). Moreover, in my view, a person who can influence others'

choices through intelligence and eloquence is more powerful than one who cannot. On this subject, see also William E. Connolly, *The Terms of Political Discourse*, 2nd ed. (Princeton: Princeton University Press, 1983), chap. 3. The various forms of power are discussed in chapter 4.

6. There is controversy over plea bargaining among scholars and lawyers, but it has not been a prominent public issue. The controversy is discussed in chapter 6.

Chapter Two
Incentives Then and Now

1. The term was introduced by Edward A. Ross in *Social Control: A Survey of the Foundations of Order* (New York: Macmillan, 1901).

2. Adam Smith, *The Theory of Moral Sentiments* (Indianapolis: Liberty Fund Press, 2009), II.ii.3.5, VII.iii.3.16.

3. Ibid., VI.ii.2.17.

4. One might think of this as a contrast between a Newtonian and a Darwinian view of the world. For more on the influence of Darwin in this period, see my "The Ethics of Incentives: Historical Origins and Contemporary Understandings," *Economics and Philosophy* 18 (April 2002): 111–39. See also note 41.

5. Frederick W. Taylor, "Shop Management," in *The Principles of Scientific Management and Shop Management* (London: Routledge/Thoemmes Press, 1993), para. 156, p. 1370; see B. F. Skinner, *Walden Two* (New York: Macmillan, 1948), vi–vii, for a similar view from behavioral psychology. John B. Watson, the founding figure of behavioral psychology, studied with Jacques Loeb, who championed a move to place the biological sciences within an engineering framework.

6. Taylor remains a controversial figure. See Daniel Nelson, *Frederick W. Taylor and the Rise of Scientific Management* (Madison: University of Wisconsin Press, 1980); and Hindy Lauer Schachter, *Frederick Taylor and the Public Administration Community: A Reevaluation* (Albany: SUNY Press, 1989).

7. Taylor, *Principles*, 10.

8. See Elton Mayo, *The Human Problems of an Industrial Civilization* (New York: Viking, 1960); Elton Mayo, *The Social Problems of an Industrial Civilization* (Boston: Harvard University Graduate School of Business, 1945); Ellen S. O'Connor, "The Politics of Management Thought: A Case Study of the Harvard Business School and the Human Relations School," *Academy of Management Review* 24,

no. 1 (1999): 117–31, 127; Lyndall F. Urwick, *The Life and Work of Elton Mayo* (London: Urwick, Orr and Partners, Ltd., 1960).

9. Schachter argues that it was unions representing skilled workers who objected to Taylorism because they were threatened by the opportunities it created for unskilled workers (*Frederick Taylor*, 55).

10. See Paul Devinat, "The American Labour Movement and Scientific Management," *International Labour Review* 13, no. 4 (1926): 461–88, 463.

11. See Samuel Haber, *Efficiency and Uplift: Scientific Management in the Progressive Era, 1890–1920* (Chicago: University of Chicago Press, 1964), esp. chap. 4.

12. Taylor, *Principles*, 26–28.

13. O'Connor, "The Politics of Management Thought," 124–25.

14. Schachter, *Frederick Taylor*, 53–55; Jill Lepore, "Not So Fast," *The New Yorker*, October 12, 2009.

15. See Robert Franklin Hoxie, *Scientific Management and Labor*, 2nd ed. (New York: D. Appleton and Co., 1921), 13–19, 169–77, for an account of trade union objections to scientific management.

16. For a very interesting history of these developments into the 1920s, see Devinat, "The American Labour Movement and Scientific Management." By the 1940s, labor was divided on the question with many supporting incentive pay as a way to increase production for the war effort. Factions on the left split. The American Communist Party supported it and the Workers Party opposed it, accusing the Communists of betraying the left under Stakhanovite influences. See C. G. Edelen, "Production with Incentive Pay" (Detroit, Mich.: Local 51, Educational Dept., UAW-CIO, 1943/44), published pamphlet; Albert Gates, "Incentive Pay: The Speed-up New Style" (New York: Workers Party, 1944/45), published pamphlet.

17. See Barry Schwartz, *The Battle for Human Nature: Science, Morality and Modern Life* (New York: W. W. Norton, 1986), 228ff.; and Barry Schwartz, Richard Schuldenfrei, and Hugh Lacey, "Operant Psychology as Factory Psychology," *Behaviorism* 6, no. 2 (1978): 229–54 for the argument that economics, factory organization, and behavioral psychology have "normalized" incentives. Incentives work, not because they appeal to certain natural characteristics, but because modern work has been organized so as to create the sort of situations in which people will be motivated by them.

18. See, e.g., Warren Atkinson, "Incentive under Socialism" (Chicago: C. H. Kerr, 1909/10), published pamphlet; J. A. Hobson, *Incentives in the New Industrial Order* (London: Leonard Parsons, 1922),

113, 143; and H. W. Laidler, "Incentives under Capitalism and Socialism" (New York: League for Industrial Democracy, 1933), published pamphlet. For an extensive bibliography of sources on this subject, see Donald Drew Egbert and Stow Persons, eds., *Socialism and American Life* (Princeton: Princeton University Press, 1952), 2:400–406.

19. Friedrich A. Hayek, ed., introduction to *Collectivist Economic Planning*, 5th ed. (1935; London: Routledge and Kegan Paul, 1956), 4.

20. Ibid., 27.

21. Ibid., 4.

22. Ibid., 8.

23. Ibid., 1–2.

24. John B. Watson, "Psychology as the Behaviorist Views It," *Psychological Review* 20, no. 2 (1913): 158–77.

25. John B. Watson, *Behaviorism* (New York: W. W. Norton, 1924), 15.

26. Ibid., 14.

27. Ibid., 11, my emphasis. The logic applied to the workplace as well. Watson asked, "After the work habits are formed, what system of changing stimuli shall we surround him with in order to keep his level of efficiency high and constantly rising?" (*Behaviorism*, 7, 9).

28. Watson was prominent, outspoken, and given to exaggeration. For contrasting views of the development of behavioral psychology and of his role in it, see John O'Donnell, *The Origins of Behaviorism: American Psychology, 1870–1920* (New York: New York University Press, 1985); A. A. Roback, *Behaviorism at Twenty-Five* (Boston: Sci-Art Publishers, 1937); and John Staddon, *The New Behaviorism: Mind, Mechanism, and Society* (Philadelphia: Psychology Press, 2000).

29. See Abram Amsel, *Behaviorism, Neobehaviorism and Cognitivism in Learning Theory: Historical and Contemporary Perspectives* (Hillsdale, NJ: Lawrence Erlbaum, 1989); C. N. Cofer and M. H. Appley, *Motivation: Theory and Research* (New York: John Wiley and Sons, 1964); and Ernest R. Hilgard and Donald G. Marquis, *Hilgard and Marquis' Conditioning and Learning*, rev. Gregory A. Kimble (1940; New York: Appleton-Century-Crofts, Inc., 1961).

30. See the sections on "incentive motivation" in Cofer and Appley, *Motivation*; and Hilgard and Marquis, *Conditioning and Learning*.

31. John A. Mills, *Control: A History of Behavioral Psychology* (New York: New York University Press, 1998). Mills notes the connection to economic language in "token economies" where experimental subjects "earn" tokens, etc. (169).

32. Watson, *Behaviorism*, 7.

33. Ibid., 104.

34. For a review of critical reaction to *Walden Two*, see Richard David Ramsey, "Morning Star: The Values-Communication of Skinner's *Walden Two*" (Ph.D. thesis, Rensselaer Polytechnic Institute, 1979), 33–46. See also Laurence Smith and William Woodward, eds., *B. F. Skinner and Behaviorism in American Culture* (Bethlehem, PA: Lehigh University Press, 1996). For an earlier debate over the merits of the new behaviorism, see John B. Watson and William MacDougall, *The Battle of Behaviorism: An Exposition and an Exposure* (New York: W. W. Norton, 1929).

35. B. F. Skinner, *About Behaviorism* (New York: A. F. Knopf, 1974), 5.

36. See note 15.

37. I am indebted to Barry Schwartz for this observation. See Schwartz, Schuldenfrei, and Lacey, "Operant Psychology as Factory Psychology" for connections between behavioral psychology and Taylorism. Staddon, *New Behaviorism*, 42ff., notes the parallels between operant psychology, which is one form of behaviorism, and contemporary economics.

38. In German, *anreiz* can be translated as "incentive" in the sense of motive or impulse, but "incentive scheme" is *leistungsabhängiges Schema*, which means something like "a scheme depending on achievement." In other words, the language for motivation and the language for reward are not the same. Similarly, in French "le motive" expresses incentive in the first sense and "primes" or "avantages" might be used to translate "incentive" in the second sense. Since 1964, the French have also used "incitation," which corresponds to the word for "incentive" in English. In Germany, the language may be changing as Germans often simply will use the English term "incentive," and "anreiz" is increasingly used as equivalent to it. According to Jesse R. Pitts, "social control is essentially an American term." See his "Social Control: The Concept," in *International Encyclopedia of the Social Sciences*, vol. 16, ed. D. L. Stills (New York: Macmillan, 1968), 381–82. William MacDougall, in his debate with Watson, stresses that "Watsonian Behaviorism is a peculiarly American product" (*Battle of Behaviorism*, 43).

39. See Dorothy Ross, *The Origins of American Social Science* (Cambridge: Cambridge University Press, 1991).

40. "The ideology of progressivism supplied psychologists with a persuasive rationale for practical relevance. Just as the successful application of science to technology and industry had resulted in a new era of prosperity, science would now be enlisted to solve the problems

of social maladjustments that rapid technological innovation and industrial expansion had caused." O'Donnell, *The Origins of Behaviorism*, 212.

41. For connections between behaviorism and Darwinism, see Schwartz, *Battle for Human Nature*, 45, 120. There were, however, at least two groups who saw social and political implications in Darwinism: "Social Darwinists," who defended inequalities as the natural result of the "survival of the fittest," and "reform Darwinists," who encouraged social intervention to accelerate the evolutionary process. I am indebted to Michael Leinisch for clarification of this distinction.

42. "Life itselfe is but Motion, and can never be without desire." Thomas Hobbes, *Leviathan*, ed. C. B. MacPherson (Harmondsworth, England: Penguin Books, 1968), 130. "I put for a generall inclination of all mankind, a perpetuall and restlesse desire of Power after power, that ceaseth only in Death" (161).

43. "Incentive contracts arise because individuals love leisure. In order to induce them to forgo some leisure, or put alternatively, to put forth effort, some form of compensation must be offered." Edward P. Lazear, "Incentive Contracts," in *The New Palgrave: A Dictionary of Economics*, ed. John Eatwell, Murray Milgate, and Peter Newman (New York: Stockton Press, 1987), 744.

44. John Winthrop, "A Model of Christian Charity," in *Winthrop Papers*, ed. Allyn Bailey Forbes et al. (Boston: Massachusetts Historical Society, 1929), 2:288.

45. The relation between incentives and habits is complex, since incentives can be used to produce habit formation in some contexts. In these cases, the incentive eventually becomes unnecessary.

46. Many Progressives advocated expanding the policymaking role of experts, including Charles Merriam, *Systematic Politics* (Chicago: University of Chicago Press, 1945), esp. chap. 10; Merriam, *New Aspects of Politics*, 3rd ed. (Chicago: University of Chicago Press, 1970); and Walter Lippmann, *The Phantom Public* (New Brunswick, NJ: Transaction Publishers, 1993), esp. chaps. 2 and 16. See also the discussion of Charles Merriam, Harold Laswell, and Walter Lippmann in O'Connor, "Politics of Management Thought," 119. Others, like John Dewey, resisted technocratic rule in favor of democratic participation. See *The Public and Its Problems* (Chicago: Swallow Press, 1954). See also Robert B. Westbrook, *John Dewey and American Democracy* (Ithaca: Cornell University Press, 1991), chap. 9; and Raymond Seidelman, *Disenchanted Realists: Political Science and the American Crisis, 1884–1984* (Albany: SUNY Press, 1985), esp. chap. 4.

47. See, e.g., Lewis Mumford, *Technics and Civilization* (New York: Harcourt, Brace and Co., 1934).

Chapter Three
"Incentives Talk"

1. See chapter 2, p. 15.

2. As we saw in the last chapter, this is precisely what behavioral psychologists like B. F. Skinner do; they deny that there is internal motivation or individual initiative of the kind I suggest.

3. Plato and Kant are classic examples.

4. For summary discussions of rational choice theory, see Jon Elster, ed., introduction to *Rational Choice* (Oxford: Basil Blackwell, 1986); Donald P. Green and Ian Shapiro, eds., *Pathologies of Rational Choice Theory* (New Haven: Yale University Press, 1994), chap. 2; and Neil J. Smelser, "The Rational Choice Perspective: A Theoretical Assessment," *Rationality and Society* 4, no. 4 (October 1992): 381–410, 386. On the sovereignty of the economic actor with respect to tastes, see p. 398. On one account, rational choice theory is a normative theory because it "tells us what we ought to do to achieve our aims," whatever they are. We ought to act rationally, adjusting our beliefs to the available evidence and so forth. Rationality also requires consistency. Elster, *Rational Choice*, 1.

5. Jon Elster takes up the issue of temptation and weakness of will, but his approach retains the subjectivism about preferences characteristic of theories of instrumental rationality. The problem is understood as a failure to maximize preference satisfaction. The question, "What should I want?" plays no role. See Elster, *Ulysses and the Sirens: Studies in Rationality and Irrationality* (Cambridge: Cambridge University Press, 1979), esp. chap. 2. Another approach is to appeal to "second-order" preferences, that is, preferences about preferences. On this view, self-control is a matter of following your second-order desires and resisting fleeting desires that contradict them. This approach also defers to the subjective attitudes of individual choosers. See, e.g., Robert E. Goodin, "Permissible Paternalism: In Defence of the Nanny State," *The Responsive Community* 1 (Summer 1991): 42–51.

6. "Nothing is said about motivation behind preferences. . . . Preferences can be based on egoistic concentration on private consumption, on altruism, on ideal principles. . . . We do not distinguish between these possibilities." Aanund Hylland, "The Purpose and Significance of Social Choice Theory: Some General Remarks and an Application

to the 'Lady Chatterly Problem,'" in *Foundations of Social Choice Theory*, ed. Jon Elster and Aanund Hylland (Cambridge: Cambridge University Press, 1986), 53. See also Amartya Sen's comment on this passage in the same volume in "Foundations of Social Choice Theory: An Epilogue," 236–37.

7. This is particularly true in research in psychology.

8. Similarly, a benefit received after the fact as a gift of appreciation is not an incentive. For example, research subjects are sometimes given gifts at the end of a study as tokens of appreciation for their participation, but these are not incentives to participate.

9. For example: "Incentives are the essence of economics. The most basic concept, demand, considers how to induce a consumer to buy more of a particular good; that is, how to give him an incentive to purchase. Similarly, supply relationships are descriptions of how agents respond with more output or labour to additional compensation." Lazear, "Incentive Contracts," 744.

10. See the preface to this book.

11. The difference between pointing out advantages and offering or promising benefits is the analogue of the difference between warnings and threats. I am grateful to an anonymous reviewer for Princeton University Press for this suggestion.

12. The stronger your "best alternative to a negotiated agreement (BATNA)," the stronger your bargaining position. The party with the most wealth or resources is not necessarily the most powerful party in the negotiation. Roger Fisher and William Ury, *Getting to Yes: Negotiating Agreement without Giving In*, 2nd ed., ed. Bruce Patton (Boston: Houghton Mifflin, 1991), 102.

13. For an excellent discussion of how viewing political institutions in a "voluntaristic framework" as structures of cooperation skews our perception of power in those institutions, see Terry M. Moe, "Power and Political Institutions," *Perspectives on Politics* 3, no. 2 (2005): 215–33.

14. Lloyd Gruber, *Ruling the World: Power Politics and the Rise of Supranational Institutions* (Princeton: Princeton University Press, 2000).

15. See Thaler and Sunstein, *Nudge*; William H. Riker, *The Art of Political Manipulation* (New Haven: Yale University Press, 1986). Riker coins the term "heresthetics" to refer to political strategies that structure the world so that you can win.

16. Jeremy Bentham, *An Introduction to the Principles of Morals and Legislation*, ed. J. H. Burns and H.L.A. Hart (New York: Athlone Press, University of London, 1970), chap. 14, paragraphs 16, 18.

17. Thaler and Sunstein, *Nudge*, 2.

Chapter Four
Ethical and Not So Ethical Incentives

1. Aristotle, *Politics*, trans. C. D. Reeve (Indianapolis: Hackett Publishing, 1998), 1253a.

2. Alexander Hamilton, James Madison, and John Jay, *The Federalist Papers*, ed. Clinton Rossiter (New York: Signet Classics, 1969), my emphasis.

3. Psychologists tend to stress that rational argument often plays a rather small role in persuasion, while philosophers are more likely to treat persuasion largely as a rational process. For the distinction between rational and non-rational forms of persuasion, see Anthony de Crespigny, "Power and Its Forms," *Political Studies* 26, no. 2 (1968): 192–205, 204–5.

4. I am indebted to Barry Schwartz for this observation.

5. Cicero, *De Officiis* (*On Duties*), trans. Walter Miller (Cambridge, MA: Loeb Classical Library, 1913), book I, 13, 41.

6. Niccolo Machiavelli, *The Prince: A New Translation, Backgrounds, Interpretations, Peripherica* (New York: Norton, 1977), chap. 18.

7. Hobbes, *Leviathan*; Michel Foucault, *Discipline and Punish: The Birth of the Prison*, 2nd ed., trans. Alan Sheridan (New York: Vintage, 1995).

8. This is the context of Smith's famous remark about the butcher and the baker. Adam Smith, *The Wealth of Nations*, ed. Edwin Cannan (Chicago: University of Chicago Press, 1976), bk.1, chap. 2, pp. 17–18. See Ruth W. Grant, *Hypocrisy and Integrity: Machiavelli, Rousseau and the Ethics of Politics* (Chicago: University of Chicago Press, 1997), 37–38.

9. For example, see the discussion of advertising in George J. Stigler and Gary S. Becker, "De Gustibus Non Disputandum," *American Economic Review* 67, no. 2 (1977): 76–90, 83–87.

10. Some international relations theorists argue that states use coercion as part of a bargaining process. Thomas Schelling developed a highly influential analysis of "coercive diplomacy," which blurs the distinction between coercion and bargaining. See Schelling, *Arms and Influence* (New Haven: Yale University Press, 1966). See also James D. Fearon on the "bargaining model of war" in "Rationalist Explanations for War," *International Organization* 49, no. 3 (1995): 379–414. The basic idea can be traced to Carl von Clausewitz's famous dictum that "war is a continuation of politics with an admixture of other means." For this interpretation of Clausewitz, see R. Harrison Wagner, *War*

and the State: The Theory of International Politics (Ann Arbor: University of Michigan Press, 2007), chap. 4.

11. Hobbes, *Leviathan*, 150.

12. These definitions were collaboratively developed in Duke University's "Persuasion Group," an informal seminar of political science faculty. I am grateful to my colleagues for their help throughout my work on this project. Compare de Crespigny, "Power and Its Forms."

13. Similarly, in discussing inducements, Conrad G. Brunk distinguishes force, hard coercion, soft coercion, and pure-and-simple offers. "The Problem of Voluntariness and Coercion in the Negotiated Plea," *Law and Society Review* 13, no. 2 (1979): 527–54, 533.

14. Compare Joseph Nye, *Soft Power: The Means to Success in World Politics* (New York: Public Affairs Press, 2004), 1–10.

15. The fact that "coercion" is used in two senses complicates matters. Defining coercion as the use or threat of force is helpful in some contexts, particularly when thinking about state power, international relations, and so forth. When the problem is to distinguish clearly between voluntary consent and coerced compliance, coercion is closer to the second meaning here—control. See chapter 5, p. 64.

16. And here I mean laws enforceable by sanctions. Every law is not coercive; consider laws allowing for tax deductions or customary international law.

17. Interestingly, the three basic categories in Figure 2 parallel those used in an encyclopedia discussion of "Social Control: Organizational Aspects" to distinguish types of organizational control: "Control may be predominantly coercive, utilitarian or normative." Each type characterizes different sorts of institutions: e.g., prisons, factories, and religious organizations, respectively. Etzioni, *International Encyclopedia of the Social Sciences*, 397.

18. While rational persuasion is consonant with liberty, "some modes of non-rational persuasion are incompatible with the autonomy of a man." de Crespigny, "Power and Its Forms," 205.

19. The first two criteria correspond to John Locke's concern with the end and origin of legitimate power. In considering the legitimacy of political, paternal, or despotic power, Locke's analysis proceeds in this way. See Locke, especially *Second Treatise*, in *Two Treatises of Government: A Critical Edition*, ed. Peter Laslett (Cambridge: Cambridge University Press, 1963), chapter 7. See also Ruth W. Grant, *John Locke's Liberalism* (Chicago: University of Chicago Press, 1987). I am well aware that the criteria I elaborate here for evaluating the uses

of power and influence are liberal ones. See the discussion of their grounding in concerns with respect for individual freedom and rationality on p. 54. For an excellent philosophic discussion of character and its importance for ethics, see Joel Kupperman, *Character* (New York: Oxford University Press, 1991).

20. Incentives may induce people to do the right thing for the wrong reason, thus undermining altruism, responsibility, or other important values. This is the critique of paying blood "donors" offered by Titmuss, *The Gift Relationship*. See also chapter 6, pp. 115–16.

21. See Thomas A. Spragens Jr., "Is the Enlightenment Project Worth Saving?" *Modern Age* 43, no. 1 (2001): 49–60, 56–57.

22. Hobbes, *Leviathan*, chaps. 17, 21.

23. Immanuel Kant, *Groundwork for the Metaphysics of Morals*, trans. James Ellington (Indianapolis: Hackett, 1981), 2–3, 11; Allen W. Wood, *Kantian Ethics* (Cambridge: Cambridge University Press, 2008), 27ff.

24. Elster, *Rational Choice*; Smelser, "The Rational Choice Perspective."

25. This is a disputed point, and many rational choice theorists do not agree with Hobbes's position.

26. Isaiah Berlin, "Two Concepts of Liberty," in *Four Essays on Liberty* (Oxford: Oxford University Press, 1969), n. 9.

27. For a fascinating study of the greater willingness of people to accept public goods than to accept money in compensation for public bads, see Carol Mansfield, George Van Houtven, and Joel Huber, "Compensating for Public Harms: Why Public Goods Are Preferred to Money," *Land Economics* 78, no. 3 (2000): 368–89. Monetary compensation is often perceived as a bribe, and people do not feel that it is respectable to accept it.

28. There is a large literature concerned with the meaning of exploitation, particularly in economic and legal contexts. See, e.g., Andrew Reeve, *Modern Theories of Exploitation* (London: Sage, 1987); John Roemer, "Should Marxists Be Interested in Exploitation?" in *Analytical Matters*, ed. John Roemer (Cambridge: Cambridge University Press, 1986); and Alan Wertheimer, *Exploitation* (Princeton: Princeton University Press, 1996). On paternalism, see Joel Feinberg, *Harm to Self* (New York: Oxford University Press, 1986), and Donald Van de Veer, *Paternalistic Intervention: The Moral Bounds on Benevolence* (Princeton: Princeton University Press, 1986).

29. Robert Taylor, "A Kantian Defense of Self-Ownership," *Journal of Political Philosophy* 12, no. 1 (2004): 65–78.

Chapter Five
Applying Standards, Making Judgments

1. This is the classic example of the use of incentives to overcome the "free rider" problem. Mancur Olson, *The Logic of Collective Action: Public Goods and the Theory of Groups* (Cambridge, MA: Harvard University Press, 1971).

2. I had originally included tax deductions for charitable giving, but see Rob Reich, "A Failure of Philanthropy: American Charity Shortchanges the Poor, and Public Policy Is Partly to Blame," *Stanford Social Innovation Review* 3, no. 4 (2005): 24–33; Reich, "Toward a Political Theory of Philanthropy," in *Giving Well: The Ethics of Philanthropy*, ed. Patricia Illingworth, Thomas Pogge, and Leif Wenar (Oxford: Oxford University Press, 2010).

3. For an interesting discussion of the more and less ethical ways such systems can be structured, see Steven D. Pearson, James E. Sabin, and Ezekiel J. Emmanuel, "Ethical Guidelines for Physician Compensation Based on Capitation," *New England Journal of Medicine* 339, no. 10 (1998): 689–93.

4. The Court did not uphold the claim in this case. See *Lori Pegram, et al., Petitioners v. Cynthia Herdrich*, 68 U.S. L. W. 4501 (June 12, 2000).

5. It may not be possible to achieve this in practice. Capitation plans have produced mixed results, both in reducing costs and in improving the quality of care. For a review of empirical evidence, see Robert H. Miller and Harold S. Luft, "Does Managed Care Lead to Better or Worse Quality of Care?" *Health Affairs* 16, no. 5 (1997): 7–25.

6. For typical disputes on the question "What counts as a voluntary transaction?" see Russell Hardin, "Blackmailing for Mutual Good," *University of Pennsylvania Law Review* 141, no. 5 (1993): 1787–1816; Leo Katz, *Ill-Gotten Gains: Evasion, Blackmail, Fraud, and Kindred Puzzles of the Law* (Chicago: University of Chicago Press, 1996); and Richard A. Posner, "The Immoralist (Review of *Ill-Gotten Gains: Evasion, Blackmail, Fraud, and Kindred Puzzles of the Law*)," *New Republic*, July 15–22, 1996, pp. 38–41 on blackmail; Kenneth Surjadinata, "Comment: Revisiting Corrupt Practices from a Market Perspective," *Emory International Law Review* 12 (Spring 1998): 1021–90 on bribery; Kenneth Kipnis, "Criminal Justice and the Negotiated Plea," *Ethics* 86, no. 2 (1976): 93–106; Alan Wertheimer, "Freedom, Morality, Plea Bargaining and the Supreme Court," *Philosophy and Public Affairs* 8, no. 3 (1979): 203–34; Ruth Macklin,

"'Due' and 'Undue' Inducements: On Paying Money to Research Subjects," *IRB* 3, no. 5 (1981): 1–6; Ruth Macklin, "Response: Beyond Paternalism," *IRB* 4, no. 3 (1982): 6–7; and Lisa Newton, "Inducement, Due and Otherwise," *IRB* 4, no. 3 (1982): 4–6, on recruitment of research subjects. On the difference between threats and offers and distinguishing voluntary consent from coercion, see G. A. Cohen, "The Structure of Proletarian Unfreedom," *Philosophy and Public Affairs* 12, no. 1 (1983): 3–33; Ruth R. Faden, Tom L. Beauchamp, and Nancy M. P. King, *A History and Theory of Informed Consent* (New York: Oxford University Press, 1986), chap. 10; Robert Nozick, "Coercion," in *Philosophy, Politics and Society*, ed. Peter Laslett, W. G. Runciman, and Quentin Skinner (Oxford: Blackwell, 1972); and Hillel Steiner, "Individual Liberty," *Proceedings of the Aristotelian Society*, n.s., 75 (1974–75): 33–50. For the distinction between coercion and exploitation, see David Zimmerman, "More on Coercive Wage Offers: A Reply to Alexander," *Philosophy and Public Affairs* 10, no. 2 (1981): part II. The literature on these questions is vast.

7. Feinberg, *Harm to Self*, 229–42.

8. It matters whether a person is choosing between two evils, for example, like the accused felon in a plea bargaining situation or the mother of the dying child (Feinberg, *Harm to Self*, 234). "'Free to choose'. . . has got to include the idea that not going along with the deal is an acceptable state of affairs." Brian Barry, "Lady Chatterly's Lover and Doctor Fisher's Bomb Party," in *Foundations of Social Choice Theory*, ed. Elster and Hylland, 26.

9. See Alan Wertheimer, *Coercion* (Princeton: Princeton University Press, 1987); and Alan Wertheimer and Franklin G. Miller, "Payment for Research Participation: A Coercive Offer?" *Journal of Medical Ethics* 34, no. 5 (2008): 389–92.

10. Barry, "Lady Chatterly's Lover and Doctor Fisher's Bomb Party," 24–25.

11. The issue of "coercive offers" is discussed further in chapter 6 at pp. 77–79, 92–93.

12. See chapter 6, p. 120, and chapter 7, pp. 129–30.

13. Studies are inconclusive on the question, but there is some consensus that companies actually make their relocation decisions on the basis of long-term fundamentals such as infrastructure and workforce characteristics and not on the basis of incentive packages. See Terry F. Buss, "The Effect of State Tax Incentives on Economic Growth and Firm Location Decisions: An Overview of the Literature," *Economic Development Quarterly* 15, no. 1 (2001): 90.

14. Federal legal cases over this issue are brought under the commerce clause. See Peter D. Enrich, "Saving the States from Themselves: Commerce Clause Constraints on State Tax Incentives for Business," *Harvard Law Review* 110, no. 2 (1996): 377–468. Michigan taxpayers joined a suit as plaintiffs against Ohio, which lured a Jeep plant through incentives.

15. Michael Walzer conceives this problem as one of dominance, where power that is legitimate in one sphere is used to gain power in an entirely different sphere. See his *Spheres of Justice: A Defense of Pluralism and Equality* (New York: Basic Books, 1983), 10–20.

16. A detailed discussion of this issue can be found in chapter 6.

17. Assume that the bonus is a pure incentive and does not serve only as compensation for the effort involved in offering the course.

18. Donors used to be much more likely to give to unrestricted funds than they are today. For a provocative discussion of these issues, see David A. Hollinger, "Money and Academic Freedom a Half-Century after McCarthyism: Universities amid the Force Fields of Capital," in *Unfettered Expression*, ed. P. G. Hollingsworth (Ann Arbor: University of Michigan Press, 2000).

Chapter Six
Getting Down to Cases

1. Alan Fiske and Phil E. Tetlock, "Taboo Trade-Offs: Constitutive Prerequisites for Social Life," in *Political Psychology: Cultural and Cross-Cultural Perspectives*, ed. Stanley A. Renshon and John Duckitt (London: MacMillan, 1999).

2. See *Sourcebook of Criminal Justice Statistics: 1999*, ed. Ann L. Pastore and Kathleen Maguire (Washington, DC: U.S. Department of Justice, Bureau of Justice Statistics, 1999), p. 429, table 5.30, p. 454, table 5.51. Trials are so rare that some attorneys are afraid to go to trial, having no trial experience, and therefore counsel defendants to accept plea agreements. David Lynch, "The Impropriety of Plea Agreements: A Tale of Two Counties," *Law and Social Inquiry* 19, no. 1 (1994): 115–33.

3. Quoted in Albert W. Alschuler, "Plea Bargaining and Its History," in *Crime and Justice in American History*, ed. Eric H. Monkkonen (London: Meckler, 1991), 3–45, 23. See also Kipnis, "Criminal Justice and the Negotiated Plea," 101.

4. *Brady v. United States*, 397 U.S. 742, 753 (1970).

5. For the constitutional standard "voluntary and intelligent," see

North Carolina v. Alford, 400 U.S. 25 (1970). For a sense of how the debate has changed, compare the special issue on plea bargaining in *Law and Society Review* 13, no. 2 (1979) with the published conference proceedings on dispute resolution in criminal law in *Marquette Law Review* 91, no. 1 (2007). See also Albert W. Alschuler, "The Changing Plea Bargaining Debate," *California Law Review* 69, no. 3 (1981): 652–730.

6. Daniel D. Barnhizer, "Bargaining Power in the Shadow of the Law: Commentary to Professors Wright and Engen, Professor Birke, and Josh Bowers," *Marquette Law Review* 91, no. 1 (2007): 123–43; Thomas W. Church Jr., "In Defense of Bargain Justice," *Law and Society Review* 13, no. 2 (1979): 509-25; Frank H. Easterbrook, "Criminal Procedure as a Market System," *Journal of Legal Studies* 12, no. 2 (1983): 289–332; Easterbrook, "Plea Bargaining as Compromise," *Yale Law Journal* 101, no. 8: Symposium on Punishment (1992): 1969–78; Milton Heumann, "Author's Reply," *Law and Society Review* 13, no. 2 (1979): 650; Robert E. Scott and William J. Stuntz, "Plea Bargaining as Contract," *Yale Law Journal* 101, no. 8: Symposium on Punishment (1992): 1909–68.

7. Alschuler, "The Changing Plea Bargaining Debate"; Albert W. Alschuler, "The Prosecutor's Role in Plea Bargaining," *University of Chicago Law Review* 36, no. 1 (1968): 50–112; Katz, *Ill-Gotten Gains*; Kipnis, "Criminal Justice and the Negotiated Plea"; Kenneth Kipnis, "A Critic's Rejoinder," *Law and Society Review* 13, no. 2 (1979): 555; Stephen J. Schulhofer, "Plea Bargaining as Disaster," *Yale Law Journal* 101, no. 8: Symposium on Punishment (1992): 1979–2009.

8. Church, "In Defense of Bargain Justice," 518.

9. On coercion and voluntariness in plea bargaining, see Brunk, "The Problem of Voluntariness and Coercion," 527; Kipnis, "Criminal Justice and the Negotiated Plea"; Michael Philips, "The Question of Voluntariness in the Plea Bargaining Controversy: A Philosophical Clarification," *Law and Society Review* 16, no. 2 (1981): 207–24; Wertheimer, *Coercion*, chap. 7; Wertheimer, "Freedom, Morality, Plea Bargaining and the Supreme Court"; Wertheimer, "The Prosecutor and the Gunman," *Ethics* 89, no. 3 (1979): 269–79. See also Katz, *Ill-Gotten Gains*, 138ff.

10. If a torturer says, "I will stop torturing you if you give me the information I want," is that a threat or an offer? Brunk, "The Problem of Voluntariness and Coercion," 542.

11. *Bordenkircher v. Hayes* 434 U.S. 358 (1978); Wertheimer, *Coercion*, 132–33.

12. This is the argument outlined in chapter 5 in the discussion of voluntariness. See p. 64.

13. Wertheimer, *Coercion*, chap. 7; Wertheimer, "Freedom, Morality, Plea Bargaining and the Supreme Court"; Wertheimer, "The Prosecutor and the Gunman," 269–79; Trebilcock, *Limits of Freedom of Contract*, chap. 4.

14. Russell Covey, "Reconsidering the Relationship between Cognitive Psychology and Plea Bargaining," *Marquette Law Review* 91, no. 1 (2007): 213–47, 242.

15. Easterbrook argues that you would expect large differentials from normal contracting in this situation ("Criminal Procedure," 311).

16. Alschuler, "The Prosecutor's Role in Plea Bargaining," 61; see Alschuler, "The Changing Plea Bargaining Debate," 684–85.

17. The Supreme Court upheld the conviction of the defendant, Alford, who pleaded guilty to second-degree murder and accepted a life sentence rather than face the possibility of the death penalty. Alford declared, "I just pleaded guilty because they said that if I didn't they would gas me for it . . . I pleaded guilty, but I'm not guilty." However, the trial judge had evidence of Alford's guilt when he accepted the plea, including the testimony of two witnesses that Alford had taken his gun from the house, declared his intention to murder the victim, and then returned declaring that he had committed the murder. *North Carolina v. Alford*, 400 U.S. 25 (1970).

18. Amy Bach, *Ordinary Injustice: How America Holds Court* (New York: Metropolitan Books, 2009), includes many illustrative examples detailing the experience of defendants.

19. This issue alone has spawned a large discussion. Several articles on the subject can be found in the *Marquette Law Review* 91, no. 1 (Fall 2007). See especially Covey, "Reconsidering the Relationship between Cognitive Psychology and Plea Bargaining." Covey argues that our psychological predispositions would be expected to lead defendants *not* to plea bargain, but the structure of the system (including large sentence differentials, pretrial detention, and what he calls "procedural brutality") is designed to counteract those dispositions.

20. See the discussion of "the innocence problem" in Scott and Stuntz, "Plea Bargaining and Contract," and Schulhofer's critique, "Plea Bargaining as Disaster."

21. Stephanos Bibas, "Plea Bargaining outside the Shadow of Trial," *Harvard Law Review* 117, no. 8 (2004): 2463–2547.

22. Douglas D. Guidorizzi, "Comment: Should We Really 'Ban' Plea Bargaining? The Core Concerns of Plea Bargaining Critics," *Emory Law Journal* 47 (Spring 1998): 753–81.

23. See Bibas, "Plea Bargaining outside the Shadow of Trial"; and Fred C. Zacharias, "Justice in Plea Bargaining," *William and Mary Law Review* 1122, no. 39 (1998): 1127–35.

24. "[A] truly convincing case against plea bargaining will require an argument that is not primarily concerned with matters having to do with the voluntariness of the choice to accept such proposals." Michael Gorr, "The Morality of Plea Bargaining," *Social Theory and Practice* 26, no. 1 (2000): 129–51, 139.

25. I am indebted to James Bourke for this point.

26. Kipnis, "Criminal Justice and the Negotiated Plea," 104.

27. Alschuler, "The Changing Plea Bargaining Debate," 669.

28. Katz, *Ill-Gotten Gains*, 255.

29. Alschuler, "The Changing Plea Bargaining Debate," 657–58.

30. Easterbrook, "Criminal Procedure," 320. His answer is that there is reason for scrutiny where one party has monopoly power, just as with unconscionable contracts.

31. Lynch, "The Impropriety of Plea Agreements."

32. Kipnis, "A Critic's Rejoinder," 560.

33. Contrast Scott and Stuntz, "Plea Bargaining as Contract," 1916, who argue that, unlike selling votes, selling your right to trial has no *social* costs.

34. Joseph Goldstein, "For Harold Laswell: Some Reflections on Human Dignity, Entrapment, Informed Consent and the Plea Bargain," *Yale Law Journal* 84, no. 4 (1975): 683–703.

35. Alschuler, "The Changing Plea Bargaining Debate," 677. See also Katz, *Ill-Gotten Gains*, 136–37.

36. Gorr, "The Morality of Plea Bargaining," 129–30; Milton Heumann, "A Note on Plea Bargaining and Case Pressure," *Law and Society Review* 9, no. 3 (1975): 515–28; John H. Langbein, "Land without Plea Bargaining: How the Germans Do It," *Michigan Law Review* 78, no. 2 (1979): 204–25; Stephen J. Schulhofer, "Is Plea Bargaining Inevitable?" *Harvard Law Review* 97, no. 5 (1984): 1037–1107; Schulhofer, "A Wake-Up Call from the Plea Bargaining Trenches," *Law and Social Inquiry* 19, no. 1 (1994): 135–44, 141–42.

37. John H. Langbein, "Torture and Plea Bargaining," *The Public Interest* 58 (Winter 1980): 43.

38. This section draws heavily on an article I coauthored with Jeremy Sugarman, "Ethics in Human Subjects Research: Do Incentives Matter?" *Journal of Medicine and Philosophy* 29, no. 6 (2004): 717–38.

39. Jonas, "Philosophical Reflections."

40. Kieran Healy argues that blood and organ procurement rates can be improved by altering procurement systems. His argument implies

that participation in research could be increased to some extent by changes in organizational approaches to recruitment and other aspects of participation. See his *Last Best Gifts: Altruism and the Market for Human Blood and Organs* (Chicago: University of Chicago Press, 2006).

41. But see G. Owen Schaefer, Ezekiel J. Emanuel, and Alan Wertheimer, "The Obligation to Participate in Biomedical Research," *Journal of the American Medical Association* 302, no. 1 (2009): 67–72. Contrast Jonas, "Philosophical Reflections," 231. There may be a moral duty, but not a legal duty, to participate in research.

42. There is some indication that incentives can be an important motivator. See C. L. Tishler and S. Bartholomae, "The Recruitment of Normal Healthy Volunteers: A Review of the Literature on the Use of Financial Incentives," *Journal of Clinical Pharmacology* 42, no. 4 (2002): 363–73. It may be true that widespread use of incentives will reduce voluntarism, though we do not know this. Unlike with blood donation, we do not have a strong tradition of voluntarism associated with becoming a research subject.

43. See chapter 3, pp. 36–38, for a discussion of the difference between rewards, compensation, and incentives.

44. For the pros and cons of various approaches, see Neal Dickert and Christine Grady, "Incentives for Research Participants," in *Oxford Textbook of Clinical Research Ethics*, ed. Ezekiel Emanuel et al. (New York: Oxford University Press, 2008), 386–95. For a discussion of wages, see Dickert and Grady, "What's the Price of a Research Subject: Approaches to Payment for Research Participation," *New England Journal of Medicine* 341, no. 3 (1999): 198–203, and James A. Anderson and Charles Weijer, "The Research Subject as Wage Earner," *Theoretical Medicine and Bioethics* 23, no. 4–5 (2002): 359–76. Anderson and Weijer challenge Dickert and Grady's recommendation that research subjects be paid an hourly wage equivalent to the wages paid to unskilled laborers. They argue that wage earners are entitled to an array of rights associated with their status as workers, including the right to overtime compensation, the right to organize, and the right to a standard work week. That is, research subjects as workers would be entitled to the same rights as other workers. What Anderson and Weijer fail to address are the duties or responsibilities that are also associated with wage labor.

45. U.S. Department of Health, Education, and Welfare, National Commission for the Protection of Human Subjects of Biomedical and Behavioral Research, *The Belmont Report: Ethical Principles and*

Guidelines for the Protection of Human Subjects of Research (Washington, DC: GPO, 1979). Note that this passage contains language suggesting elements of each of the two forms of undue influence we distinguished above: "Unjustifiable pressures usually occur when persons in positions of authority or commanding influence ... urge a course of action for a subject" and "Undue influence ... occurs through an offer of an excessive, unwarranted, inappropriate or improper reward or other overture in order to obtain compliance." It also includes one case that we would classify as blackmail: threatening to withdraw health services. See chapter 5, p. 71.

46. World Medical Association, *Declaration of Helsinki*, http://www.wma.net/en/30publications/10policies/b3/17c.pdf.

47. Jeffrey P. Kahn, Anna M. Mastroianni, and Jeremy Sugarman, eds., *Beyond Consent: Seeking Justice in Research* (New York: Oxford University Press, 1998).

48. Of course, if you have a degenerative disease, you will get sicker if you do not agree to participate in a research study that may be the only way to access a potentially beneficial treatment. But your worsened condition will be the result of the natural history of the disease, not the result of refusing the offer, as would be the case with blackmail.

49. For an alternative view, see Wertheimer and Miller, "Payment for Research Participation." See also Ezekiel J. Emanuel, "Ending Concerns about Undue Inducement," *American Society of Law and Medicine* 32, no. 1 (2004): 100–106. Alex J. London replies with "Undue Inducements and Reasonable Risks: Will the Dismal Science Lead to Dismal Research Ethics?" *American Journal of Bioethics* 5, no. 5 (2005): 29–32.

50. Macklin, "'Due' and 'Undue' Inducements"; Newton, "Inducement, Due and Otherwise"; Macklin, "Response: Beyond Paternalism"; Tom L. Beauchamp, Bruce Jennings, Eleanor D. Kinney, and Robert J. Levine, "Pharmaceutical Research Involving the Homeless," *Journal of Medicine and Philosophy* 27, no. 5 (2002): 547–64. A similar tension is found in M. Wilkinson and A. Moore, "Inducement in Research," *Bioethics* 11, no. 5 (1997): 373–89; and Paul McNeill, "A Response to Wilkinson and Moore: Paying People to Participate in Research: Why Not?" *Bioethics* 11, no. 5 (1997): 390–96.

51. On irresistible offers, see Faden, Beauchamp, and King, *History and Theory of Informed Consent*, chap. 10.

52. Newton, "Inducement, Due and Otherwise." See also Beauchamp et al., "Pharmaceutical Research," 549: "to categorically exclude

subjects from participation in research would constitute an unjustifiable violation of their rights." Of course, forbidding the use of incentives does not prevent anyone from volunteering.

53. Wertheimer and Miller, "Payment for Research Participation," 391.

54. See chapter 5, footnote 10, on p. 65 and accompanying text. See Faden, Beauchamp, and King, *A History and Theory of Informed Consent*, 357–59, where the distinction is made between "welcome" and "unwelcome" offers. The distinction is important and resembles mine. But the authors adhere to the sole criterion of voluntariness, arguing, mistakenly I believe, that a choice to accept an "unwelcome" offer is not an autonomous action.

55. Some would certainly argue that to say "I did it against my better judgment" is an incoherent statement. Whatever you did was what you chose do to; it was the result of your judgment. According to this view, it is equally incoherent to say that "I did it against my will." When the robber offers you a choice of your money or your life, surrendering your money is still a choice. Coercion as it is ordinarily understood disappears as a meaningful category. If one takes the position that every action is necessarily a voluntary action (short of being literally physically overpowered), one particularly needs to be able to distinguish in some other language between types of voluntary actions in order to be true to human experience. To choose with a gun to your head is experienced quite differently than choices that are made in the absence of threats. Ethical argument needs to recognize the distinction in one way or another. See also the discussion of Hobbes in chapter 4, p. 54.

56. Less directly and less dramatically, though in a similar category, large payments for eggs or sperm function as seductive offers for people with religious convictions opposed to in vitro fertilization. Those individuals are morally obliged to reject such offers. See note 58.

57. R. M. Nelson, "Children as Research Subjects," in *Beyond Consent*, ed. Kahn, Mastroianni, and Sugarman, 47–66.

58. There are always two sides to the coin: the ethics of offering an incentive and the ethics of accepting or rejecting it. Our concern here is with the former, but we should remember that the parents in this case faced an ethical dilemma as well. One way to view the offer is as an attempt to corrupt the parents.

59. Anne Drapkin Lyerly, Margaret Olivia Little, and Ruth Faden, "The Second Wave: Toward Responsible Inclusion of Pregnant Women in Research," *International Journal of Feminist Approaches to Bio-*

ethics 1, no. 2 (2008): 6–22; Anne Drapkin Lyerly, Lisa M. Mitchell, Elizabeth M. Armstrong, Lisa H. Harris, Rebecca Kukla, Miriam Kupperman, and Margaret Olivia Little, "Risks, Values, and Decision Making Surrounding Pregnancy," *Obstetrics and Gynecology* 109, no. 4 (2007): 979–84.

60. This issue is discussed in J. D. Moreno, "Convenient and Captive Populations," in *Beyond Consent*, ed. Kahn, Mastroianni, and Sugarman, 111–30.

61. This is similar to Titmuss's concern that incentives will undermine the collective commitment to altruism as a value (see p. 4). For a related argument, see D. Nelkin and L. Andrews, "Homo Economicus: Commercialization of Body Tissue in the Age of Biotechnology," *Hastings Center Report* 28 (1998): 30–39.

62. S. R. Benatar, "Reflections and Recommendations on Research Ethics in Developing Countries," *Social Science and Medicine* 54, no. 7 (2002): 1131–41; Ezekiel J. Emanuel, Xolani E. Currie, and Alan Herman, "Undue Inducement in Clinical Research in Developing Countries: Is It a Worry?" *Lancet* 366, no. 9482 (2005): 336–40.

63. G. Corbie-Smith, S. B. Thomas, and D. M. St. George, "Distrust, Race, and Research," *Archives of Internal Medicine* 162, no. 21 (2002): 2458–63.

64. I focus on the report's other adjectives: "unwarranted, inappropriate, or improper" inducements.

65. Cynthia E. Cryder, Alex J. London, Kevin G. Volpp, and George Loewenstein, "Informative Inducement: Study Payment as a Signal of Risk," *Social Science and Medicine* 70, no. 3 (2010): 455–64.

66. The first big change came in the early 1970s when the system of gold reserves was abandoned and IMF loans were no longer needed to maintain fixed exchange rates. James Vreeland, "The IMF and Economic Development," in *Reinventing Foreign Aid*, ed. William Easterly (Cambridge, MA: MIT Press, 2008), 355.

67. Martin Feldstein, "Refocusing the IMF," *Foreign Affairs* 77, no. 2 (1998): 20–33, 20–22; Vreeland, "IMF and Economic Development," 354–55; IMF, "IMF Adopts Guidelines Regarding Governance Issues," IMF News Brief No. 97/15, August 4, 1997, http://www.imf.org/external/np/sec/nb/1997/nb9715.htm.

68. Strom C. Thacker, "The High Politics of IMF Lending," *World Politics* 52, no. 1 (1999): 38–75; James Vreeland, *The International Monetary Fund: Politics of Conditional Lending* (London: Routledge, 2007), 48; Thomas D. Willett, "Understanding the IMF Debate," *The Independent Review* 5, no. 4 (2001): 593–610, 599.

69. Christian Barry and Lydia Tomitova, "Fairness in Sovereign Debt," *Ethics in International Affairs* 21, no. 1 (2007): 41–79, 56, 60; Sanjay G. Reddy, "International Debt: The Constructive Implications of Some Moral Mathematics," *Ethics and International Affairs* 21, no. 1 (2007): 81–92, 83–88; Jeffrey Sachs, "Conditionality, Debt Relief, and the Developing Country Debt Crisis" (working paper no. 2644, National Bureau of Economic Research, 1988), 14.

70. Thucydides, *History of the Peloponnesian War*, trans. Rex Warner (Harmondsworth, England: Penguin Books, 1972), book V, para. 89.

71. Vreeland, "IMF and Economic Development," 356.

72. The same argument is made with respect to conditions attached to foreign aid. See Olav Stokke, ed., *Aid and Political Conditionality* (London: Frank Cass, 1995), 9.

73. Thomas Donaldson, "The Ethics of Conditionality in International Debt," *Millennium: Journal of International Studies* 20, no. 2 (1991): 155–68, 163; Tony Killick, Ramani Gunatilaka, and Anna Marr, *Aid and the Political Economy of Policy Change* (London: Routledge, 1998), 12–17; Sachs, "Conditionality, Debt Relief, and the Developing Country Debt Crisis," 6–7; Vreeland, *The International Monetary Fund*, 62–67.

74. This is a typical "moral hazard" problem.

75. Feldstein, "Refocusing the IMF," 27.

76. Jacqueline Best, "The Moral Politics of IMF Reforms: Universal Economics, Particular Ethics," *Perspectives on Global Development and Technology* 4, no. 3–4 (2005): 357–78, 373.

77. My emphasis. Though the article was not referring to an IMF bailout, the issue remains the same. Floyd Norris, "Fraying at the Edges," *New York Times*, February 4, 2010, p. 8 of the Business section.

78. Feldstein, "Refocusing the IMF," offers a powerful critique of IMF conditionality in South Korea along these lines.

79. Vivien Collingwood, "Assistance with Fewer Strings Attached," *Ethics in International Affairs* 17, no. 1 (2003): 55–67; William Easterly, *The White Man's Burden: Why the West's Efforts to Aid the Rest Have Done So Much Ill and So Little Good* (Oxford: Oxford University Press, 2006), 192; Vreeland, *The International Monetary Fund*, 130; Willett, "Understanding the IMF Debate," 600ff., 607–8.

80. IMF "Guidelines Regarding Governance Issues"; IMF, "Conditionality in Fund-Supported Programs—Policy Issues," February 20, 2001, http://www.imf.org/external/np/pdr/cond/2001/eng/overview; IMF, "Guidelines on Conditionality," September 25, 2002, http://www.imf.org/external/np/pdr/cond/2002/eng/guid/092302.pdf; IMF, "Factsheet—IMF

Conditionality," September 27, 2010, http://www.imf.org/external/np/exr/facts/conditio.htm.

81. In line with these principles, the IMF has introduced two programs that significantly relax conditionality, though they do not eliminate it. "Modernized conditionality" uses preset qualification criteria rather than performance reviews to assess loan eligibility. The "Flexible Credit Line" program makes nonconditional funds available to countries that qualify in advance because of "strong fundamentals." IMF, "IMF Overhauls Lending Framework," press release, March 24, 2009; http://www.imf.org/external/np/sec/pr/2009/pr0985.htm.

82. Best, "The Moral Politics of IMF Reforms," 373; Joseph E. Stiglitz, "Ethics, Market and Government Failure, and Globalization," in *Sovereign Debt at the Crossroads*, ed. Chris Jochnick and Fraser A. Preston (Oxford: Oxford University Press, 2006), 158–74, 2; Vreeland, "IMF and Economic Development," 355, 367.

83. Easterly, *White Man's Burden*, 206.

84. Killick, Gunatilaka, and Marr, *Aid and the Political Economy of Policy Change*, 16; Ann Pettifor, "Resolving International Debt Crises Fairly," *Ethics and International Affairs* 17, no. 2 (2003): 2–9; Reddy, "International Debt," 92; Bernard Snoy, "Ethical Issues in International Lending," *Journal of Business Ethics* 8, no. 8 (1989): 635–39; Stiglitz, "Ethics, Market and Government Failure, and Globalization," 1–3.

85. Easterly, *White Man's Burden*, on political instability, see pp. 191–94, on accountability, see pp. 206–7.

86. Vreeland, "The IMF and Economic Development," esp. 365–66; Vreeland, *The International Monetary Fund*, 94. See also Killick, Gunatilaka, and Marr, *Aid and the Political Economy of Policy Change*, for an assessment of effects of aid conditionality on growth. See also William Easterly, *The Elusive Quest for Growth: Economists' Adventures and Misadventures in the Tropics* (Cambridge, MA: MIT Press, 2002).

87. E.g., see Willett, "Understanding the IMF Debate"; David Dollar and Jacob Svensson, "What Explains the Success or Failure of Structural Adjustment Programmes?" *Economic Journal* 110, no. 466 (2000): 894–917; and Michel Camdessus, "The International Monetary Fund in a Globalized World Economy: The Tasks Ahead," in *At the Global Crossroads: The Sylvia Ostry Foundation Lectures*, ed. Sylvia Ostry (Montreal: Institute for Research on Public Policy, 2003). For a more general argument extolling "laissez-faire" policies and the benefits of globalization, see David Dollar and Aart Kraay, "Spreading the Wealth," *Foreign Affairs* 81, no. 1 (2002): 120–33.

88. Major voices include Charles Beitz, *The Idea of Human Rights* (Oxford: Oxford University Press, 2009); Paul Collier, *The Bottom Billion: Why the Poorest Countries Are Failing and What Can Be Done about It* (Oxford: Oxford University Press, 2007); Martha Nussbaum, *Frontiers of Justice: Disability, Nationality, Species Membership* (Cambridge, MA: Harvard University Press, 2006), esp. chaps. 4–5; Thomas Pogge, *World Poverty and Human Rights* (Malden, MA: Polity Press, 2008); John Rawls, *The Law of Peoples* (Cambridge, MA: Harvard University Press, 1999), esp. 105–13; and Joseph E. Stiglitz, *Globalization and Its Discontents* (New York: W. W. Norton, 2002). For general discussions of the debate, see Best, "The Moral Politics of IMF Reforms"; and Helen V. Milner, "Review: Globalization, Development, and International Institutions: Normative and Positive Perspectives," *Perspectives on Politics* 3, no. 4 (2005): 833–54.

89. Collier, *The Bottom Billion*, 110; Thomas Pogge, "The Moral Demands of Global Justice," *Dissent* 47, no. 4 (2000): 37–42, 41–42; Snoy, "Ethical Issues in International Lending," 637.

90. Vreeland, "IMF and Economic Development," 369.

91. Karen L. Remmer, "The Politics of Economic Stabilization: IMF Standby Programs in Latin America, 1954–1984," *Comparative Politics* 19, no. 1 (1986): 1–24, 21.

92. Vreeland, *The International Monetary Fund*, 110.

93. Collier, *The Bottom Billion*; Killick, Gunatilaka, and Marr, *Aid and the Political Economy of Policy Change*; George Sorenson, "Conditionality, Democracy and Development," in *Aid and Political Conditionality*, ed. Olav Stokke (London: Frank Cass, 1995).

94. He contrasts Planners with Searchers, who have opposite characteristics in every respect. See Easterly, *White Man's Burden*, 5–7 and chap. 6.

95. Debates over how to strike the balance between these purposes can be heated. "High-stakes testing" was implemented in part by those who believed that cognitive development had been getting short shrift.

96. Roland Fryer quoted by Julian Liam in a *Washington Post* editorial, "But Wrong on Paying Students," Sunday, August 31, 2008. Professor Fryer, a Harvard economist, is a major force behind these programs.

97. For a general discussion of these perverse effects, see Barry Schwartz, *The Costs of Living: How Market Freedom Erodes the Best Things in Life* (New York: W. W. Norton, 1994), especially chap. 8, "The 'Debasing' of Work," and chapter 9, "The Demeaning of Education: Turning Play into Work."

98. See chapter 3, p. 43.

99. Mills, *Control*, 165–78.

100. Tim Urdan, "Intrinsic Motivation, Extrinsic Rewards, and Divergent Views of Reality," *Educational Psychology Review* 15, no. 3 (2003): 311–25, 321–24.

101. Samuel Bowles reviews forty-one studies in "Policies Designed for Self-Interested Citizens May Undermine 'The Moral Sentiments': Evidence from Economic Experiments," *Science* 320, no. 5883 (2008): 1605–9.

102. Carl Mellström and Magnus Johannesson, "Crowding Out in Blood Donation: Was Titmuss Right?" *Journal of the European Economic Association* 6, no. 4 (2008): 845–63.

103. Bruno D. Frey, *Not Just for the Money: An Economic Theory of Personal Motivation* (Cheltenham, UK: Edward Elgar, 1997), chap. 8, with Felix Oberholzer-Gee. See also Mansfield, Van Houtven, and Huber, "Compensating for Public Harms."

104. Dan Ariely, "What's the Value of a Big Bonus?" *New York Times*, November 20, 2008.

105. Jack W. Brehm, *A Theory of Psychological Reactance* (New York: Academic Press, 1966), 81–90.

106. For summaries of some of this research, see Edward L. Deci and Richard M. Ryan, *Intrinsic Motivation and Self-Determination in Human Behavior* (New York: Plenum Press, 1985), 262–63; Kenneth O. McGraw, "The Detrimental Effects of Reward on Performance: A Literature Review and a Prediction Model," in *The Hidden Costs of Reward: New Perspectives on the Psychology of Human Motivation*, ed. Mark Lepper and David Greene (Hillsdale, NJ: Lawrence Erlbaum, 1978), 33–60; and Daniel H. Pink, *Drive: The Surprising Truth about What Motivates Us* (New York: Riverhead Books, 2009), part I.

107. For examples, see Edward L. Deci, John Nezlek, and Louise Sheinman, "Characteristics of the Rewarder and Intrinsic Motivation of the Rewardee," *Journal of Personality and Social Psychology* 40, no. 1 (1981): 3–10; Cheryl Flink, Ann K. Boggiano, Deborah S. Main, Mary Barrett, and Phyllis A. Katz, "Children's Achievement-Related Behaviors: The Role of Extrinsic and Intrinsic Motivational Orientations," in *Achievement and Motivation: A Social-Development Perspective*, ed. Ann K. Boggiano and Thane S. Pittman (Cambridge: Cambridge University Press, 1993), 189–214; and Mark R. Lepper, David Greene, and Richard E. Nisbet, "Undermining Children's Intrinsic Interest with Extrinsic Rewards," *Journal of Personality Psychology* 28, no. 1 (1973): 129–37. For essays on the current state of the discussion, see Carol Sansone and Judith M. Harackiewicz, eds.,

Intrinsic and Extrinsic Motivation: The Search for Optimal Motivation and Performance (San Diego: Academic Press, 2000). There is a series of exchanges over the research findings that began with a meta-analysis by Judith Cameron and W. David Pierce showing that rewards do not significantly decrease intrinsic motivation. Their work was challenged by Edward Deci, Richard Koestner, and Richard Ryan. The exchange begins in vol. 64, 1994, and continues in vol. 66, 1996, and vol. 71, 2001, of the *Review of Educational Research*. I believe that Deci, Koestner, and Ryan get the better of the argument.

108. Bowles, "Policies Designed for Self-Interested Citizens"; Frey, *Not Just for the Money*, part 1; Titmuss, *The Gift Relationship*, 157, 223.

109. Frey, *Not Just for the Money*, chap. 5; Titmuss, *The Gift Relationship*, 198–99.

110. Robert H. Frank, Thomas Gilovich, and Dennis T. Regan, "Does Studying Economics Inhibit Cooperation?" *Journal of Economic Perspectives* 7, no. 2 (1993): 159–72. See also Dale T. Miller, "The Norm of Self-Interest," *American Psychologist* 54, no. 12 (1999): 1053–60.

111. Titmuss, *The Gift Relationship*, 75–77. This is also a concern with paying medical research subjects.

112. Brian A. Jacob and Stephen D. Levitt, "Rotten Apples: An Investigation of the Prevalence and Predictors of Teacher Cheating," *Quarterly Journal of Economics* 118, no. 3 (2003): 843–77; Jacob and Levitt, "Catching Cheating Teachers: The Results of an Unusual Experiment in Implementing Theory," in *Brookings-Wharton Papers on Urban Affairs*, ed. William G. Gale and Janet Rothenberg Pack (Washington, DC: Brookings Institution Press, 2003), 185–209. For a summary discussion, see Steven D. Levitt and Stephen J. Dubner, *Freakonomics: A Rogue Economist Explores the Hidden Side of Everything* (New York: Harper Collins, 2005), 24–38.

113. Eric M. Anderman, Tripp Griesinger, and Gloria Westerflield, "Motivation and Cheating during Early Adolescence," *Journal of Educational Psychology* 90, no. 1 (1998): 84–93; Carol Midgley, Avi Kaplan, and Michael Middleton, "Performance-Approach Goals: Good for What, for Whom, under What Circumstances, and at What Cost?" *Journal of Educational Psychology* 93, no. 1 (2001): 77–86, 82.

114. Alasdair MacIntyre, *After Virtue* (Notre Dame, IN: Notre Dame University Press, 1981), 163.

115. Margaret Raymond shows different results for reading and for math in "Paying for A's: An Early Exploration of Student Reward and Incentive Programs in Charter Schools" (paper presented at the

CESifo/PEPG Conference "Economic Incentives: Do They Work in Education? Insights and Findings from Behavioral Research," Munich, May 16–17, 2008). For a useful review article, see Robert E. Slavin, "Can Financial Incentives Enhance Educational Outcomes? Evidence from International Experiments" (unpublished paper, Institute for Effective Education, University of York, 2009).

116. Margaret B. Spencer, Elizabeth Noll, and Elaine Cassidy, "Monetary Incentives in Support of Academic Achievement: Results of a Randomized Field Trial Involving High-Achieving, Low-Resource, Ethnically Diverse Urban Adolescents," *Evaluation Review* 29, no. 3 (2005): 199–222. See Slavin, "Can Financial Incentives Enhance Educational Outcomes," 1.

117. An exception is C. Kirabo Jackson, "A Stitch in Time: The Effects of a Novel Incentive-Based High-School Intervention on College Outcomes" (working paper 15722, National Bureau of Economic Research, 2010), http://www.nber.org/papers/w15722.pdf.

118. Roland Fryer's work is the most ambitious attempt to date to determine the effects of financial incentives programs on student performance, and it, too, shows mixed results (although *Time* magazine reported that the research showed that the incentives worked; see Amanda Ripley, "Should Kids Be Bribed to Do Well in School?" *Time*, April 19, 2010). See Fryer, "Financial Incentives and Student Achievement: Evidence from Randomized Trials," (working paper 15898, National Bureau of Economic Research, 2010), http://www.nber.org/papers/w15898. Fryer conducted four sets of experiments in different cities. Only one of the programs yielded statistically significant, positive effects on test scores and grades. Moreover, Fryer's experiments do not offer longitudinal data, which is crucial for assessing the impact of incentives on students' motivation.

119. Ruth W. Grant and Nathan Tarcov, eds., *John Locke: Some Thoughts Concerning Education and Of the Conduct of the Understanding* (Indianapolis: Hackett, 1996), esp. paragraphs 42–52, 56–62, 71–72, 149–50.

120. Marilyn Ornstein, Duke School for Children, Durham, NC.

121. Pink, *Drive*, 38–39.

122. Chapter 3, p. 36.

123. Bowles, "Policies Designed for Self-Interested Citizens," 1608; Samuel Bowles, "When Economic Incentives Backfire," *Harvard Business Review* 87, no. 3 (2009): 8b.

124. A note of caution on this point: it is easy for people who are comfortably well-off to worry about encouraging materialism. People

often have perfectly good reasons to concern themselves with material things.

125. Gary T. Henry and Ross Rubenstein, "Paying for Grades: Impact of Merit-Based Financial Aid on Educational Quality," *Journal of Policy Analysis and Management* 21, no. 1 (2002): 93–109; Judith Scott-Clayton, "On Money and Motivation: A Quasi-Experimental Analysis of Financial Incentives for College Achievement" (unpublished paper, Columbia University Teachers College, 2009). Both studies show positive effects of financial aid for college as an incentive for improved performance.

126. This is an important element of all of the critiques cited here: Bowles, "Policies Designed for Self-Interested Citizens" and "When Economic Incentives Backfire"; Brehm, *A Theory of Psychological Reactance*; Deci and Ryan, *Intrinsic Motivation and Self-Determination in Human Behavior*; Frey, "Constitution for Knaves," "Institutions and Morale," and *Not Just for the Money*; and Pink, *Drive*. Alfie Kohn, one of the strongest critics of incentives, writes, "pop behaviorism is by its very nature dehumanizing." See his *Punished by Rewards: The Trouble with Gold Stars, Incentive Plans, A's, Praise and Other Bribes* (New York: Houghton Mifflin, 1993), 25.

127. The same can be said for incentives in the workplace. Several authors draw implications for employer-employee relations from the same psychological research that informs the debate over incentives in education. See especially Bowles, "Policies Designed for Self-Interested Citizens"; Pink, *Drive*; and Kohn, *Punished by Rewards*, chap. 7.

Chapter Seven
Beyond Voluntariness

1. Rosaline Ziegler, conversation with the author, American Association of Sex Educators, Counselors and Therapists, Miami, FL, May 2002.

2. An agreement can be exploitative even when both parties consent. See Wertheimer, *Exploitation*, 247–53.

3. Rational choice theorists would consider the second type of legislative bargain a special case of the third type. See, e.g., Emerson M. S. Niou and Peter C. Ordeshook, "Universalism in Congress," *American Journal of Political Science* 29, no. 2 (1985): 246–58; and Barry Weingast, "A Rational Choice Perspective on Congressional Norms," *American Journal of Political Science* 23, no. 2 (1979): 245–62. See Avishai Margalit, *Compromises and Rotten Compromises* (Princeton:

Princeton University Press, 2009), chap. 2, for the limitations of game theory in explaining compromises that involve recognition.

4. Berlin, "Two Concepts of Liberty," 131, my emphasis. Berlin goes on to discuss the dangers of this conception for politics.

5. Brehm, *A Theory of Psychological Reactance.*

6. These are two different reactions often conflated in discussions of crowding out. Bowles, "Policies Designed for Self-Interested Citizens," offers three additional explanations, besides threats to autonomy, to explain crowding out. Incentives can signal that self-interested behavior is appropriate; they have "learning effects," inducing self-interested behavior over time; and they convey information about whether or not the target of the incentive is trusted or respected. I consider this last as an issue of autonomy as well.

7. John Dempsey, president of Sandhills, "Taste of College Keeps Students in High School," *New York Times*, February 8, 2010, p. A14.

8. Tracy Meares, quoted in Jeffrey Rosen, "Prisoners of Parole," *New York Times Magazine*, January 10, 2010, pp. 37–39. David Kennedy, John Jay College of Criminal Justice, is a leading proponent of the new deterrence.

9. George Akerlof and Rachel Kranton, *Identity Economics* (Princeton: Princeton University Press, 2010), chap. 5.

10. Bruno Frey, "Institutions and Morale: The Crowding Out Effect," in *Economics, Values and Organizations,* ed. A. Ben-Ner and L. Putterman (Cambridge: Cambridge University Press, 1998), 437–60, 452–54; Frey, "A Constitution for Knaves Crowds Out Civic Virtues," *Economic Journal* 107, no. 443 (1997): 1043–53, 1050–52.

11. Deci and Ryan, *Intrinsic Motivation and Self-Determination in Human Behavior.*

12. Frey, *Not Just for the Money.*

13. Ernst Fehr and Armin Falk, "Psychological Foundations of Incentives" (working paper no. 95, Working Paper Series ISSN 1424-0459, Institute for Empirical Research in Economics, University of Zurich, November 2001).

14. Staddon, *Behaviorism,* 42ff.

Chapter Eight
A Different Kind of Conversation

1. Of course, they are also viewed as more efficient.

2. For an excellent discussion of this tradition in American liberalism, see Thomas A. Spragens Jr., *Getting the Left Right: The Transformation,*

Decline, and Reformation of American Liberalism (Lawrence: University Press of Kansas, 2009), chap. 1.

3. Frey, "Institutions and Morale," includes among "noncalculative motives": morale, public spirit, social capital, trust, and intrinsic motivation.

4. See Frey, "Constitution for Knaves."

5. Of course, the decision to employ incentives may involve deliberation among the decision-makers. But the relevant point with respect to democratic values is that this is an exclusive conversation.

6. Ruth W. Grant, "Passions and Interests Revisited: The Psychological Foundations of Economics and Politics," *Public Choice* 137, no. 3/4 (2008): 451–61.

7. Samuel Bowles, *Machiavelli's Mistake: Why Good Laws Are No Substitute for Good Citizens* (New Haven: Yale University Press, 2011).

8. See Westbrook, *John Dewey and American Democracy*, chap. 9. For a contemporary discussion raising some of the same issues, see Amartya Sen, *Development as Freedom* (New York: Anchor Books, 1999).

References

Akerlof, George, and Rachel Kranton. *Identity Economics*. Princeton: Princeton University Press, 2010.

Alschuler, Albert W. "The Prosecutor's Role in Plea Bargaining." *University of Chicago Law Review* 36, no. 1 (1968): 50–112.

———. "The Changing Plea Bargaining Debate." *California Law Review* 69, no. 3 (1981): 652–730.

———. "Plea Bargaining and Its History." In *Crime and Justice in American History*, ed. Eric H. Monkkonen. London: Meckler, 1991.

Amsel, Abram. *Behaviorism, Neobehaviorism and Cognitivism in Learning Theory: Historical and Contemporary Perspectives*. Hillsdale, NJ: Lawrence Erlbaum, 1989.

Anderman, Eric M., Tripp Griesinger, and Gloria Westerflield. "Motivation and Cheating during Early Adolescence." *Journal of Educational Psychology* 90, no. 1 (1998): 84–93.

Anderson, James A., and Charles Weijer. "The Research Subject as Wage Earner." *Theoretical Medicine and Bioethics* 23, no. 4–5 (2002): 359–76.

Ariely, Dan. "What's the Value of a Big Bonus?" *New York Times*, November 20, 2008, p. 43.

Aristotle. *Politics*. Trans. C. D. Reeve. Indianapolis: Hackett, 1998.

Arrow, Kenneth. "Gifts and Exchanges." *Philosophy and Public Affairs* 1, no. 4 (1972): 343–62.

Atkinson, Warren. "Incentive under Socialism." Chicago: C. H. Kerr, 1910.

Bach, Amy. *Ordinary Injustice: How America Holds Court*. New York: Metropolitan Books, 2009.

Barnhizer, Daniel D. "Bargaining Power in the Shadow of the Law: Commentary to Professors Wright and Engen, Professor Birke, and Josh Bowers." *Marquette Law Review* 91, no. 1 (2007): 123–43.

Barry, Brian. "Lady Chatterly's Lover and Doctor Fisher's Bomb Party." In *Foundations of Social Choice Theory*, ed. Jon Elster and Aanund Hylland. Cambridge: Cambridge University Press, 1986.

Barry, Christian, and Lydia Tomitova. "Fairness in Sovereign Debt." *Ethics and International Affairs* 21, no. 1 (2007): 41–79.

Beauchamp, Tom L., Bruce Jennings, Eleanor D. Kinney, and Robert J. Levine. "Pharmaceutical Research Involving the Homeless." *Journal of Medicine and Philosophy* 27, no. 5 (2002): 547–64.

Beitz, Charles. *The Idea of Human Rights.* Oxford: Oxford University Press, 2009.

Benatar, S. R. "Reflections and Recommendations on Research Ethics in Developing Countries." *Social Science and Medicine* 54, no. 7 (2002): 1131–41.

Bentham, Jeremy. *An Introduction to the Principles of Morals and Legislation,* ed. J. H. Burns and H.L.A. Hart. New York: Athlone Press, University of London, 1970.

Berlin, Isaiah. "Two Concepts of Liberty." In *Four Essays on Liberty.* Oxford: Oxford University Press, 1969.

Best, Jacqueline. "The Moral Politics of IMF Reforms: Universal Economics, Particular Ethics." *Perspectives on Global Development and Technology* 4, no. 3–4 (2005): 357–78.

Bibas, Stephanos. "Plea Bargaining outside the Shadow of Trial." *Harvard Law Review* 117, no. 8 (2004): 2463–2547.

Bowles, Samuel. "Policies Designed for Self-Interested Citizens May Undermine 'The Moral Sentiments': Evidence from Economic Experiments." *Science* 320, no. 5883 (2008): 1605–9.

———. "When Economic Incentives Backfire." *Harvard Business Review* 87, no. 3 (2009): 8b–c.

———. *Machiavelli's Mistake: Why Good Laws Are No Substitute for Good Citizens.* New Haven: Yale University Press, 2011.

Brehm, Jack W. *A Theory of Psychological Reactance.* New York: Academic Press, 1966.

Brunk, Conrad G. "The Problem of Voluntariness and Coercion in the Negotiated Plea." *Law and Society Review* 13, no. 2 (1979): 527–54.

Buss, Terry F. "The Effect of State Tax Incentives on Economic Growth and Firm Location Decisions: An Overview of the Literature." *Economic Development Quarterly* 15, no. 1 (2001): 90–105.

Camdessus, Michel. "The International Monetary Fund in a Globalized World Economy: The Tasks Ahead." In *At the Global Crossroads: The Sylvia Ostry Foundation Lectures,* ed. Sylvia Ostry. Montreal: Institute for Research on Public Policy, 2003.

Cameron, Judy. "Negative Effects of Reward on Intrinsic Motivation: A Limited Phenomenon: Comment on Deci, Koestner, and Ryan." *Review of Educational Research* 71, no. 1 (2001): 29–42.

Cameron, Judith, and W. David Pierce. "The Debate about Rewards and Intrinsic Motivation: Protests and Accusations Do Not Alter the Results." *Review of Educational Research* 66, no. 1 (1996): 39–51.

———. "Reinforcement, Reward, and Intrinsic Motivation: A Meta-analysis." *Review of Educational Research* 64, no. 3 (1994): 363–423.

Church, Thomas W., Jr. "In Defense of Bargain Justice." *Law and Society Review* (special issue on plea bargaining) 13, no. 2 (1979): 509–25.

Cialdini, Robert B. *Influence: Science and Practice*. 5th ed. Boston: Pearson, 2009.

Cicero, Marcus T. *De Officiis (On Duties)*. Trans. Walter Miller. Cambridge, MA: Loeb Classical Library, 1913.

Cofer, C. N., and M. H. Appley. *Motivation: Theory and Research*. New York: John Wiley and Sons, 1964.

Cohen, G. A. "The Structure of Proletarian Unfreedom." *Philosophy and Public Affairs* 12, no. 1 (1983): 3–33

———. "Robert Nozick and Wilt Chamberlain: How Patterns Preserve Liberty." *Erkenntnis* 11 (1997): 5–23.

Collier, Paul. *The Bottom Billion: Why the Poorest Countries Are Failing and What Can Be Done about It*. Oxford: Oxford University Press, 2007.

Collingwood, Vivien. "Assistance with Fewer Strings Attached." *Ethics in International Affairs* 17, no. 1 (2003): 55–67.

Connolly, William E. *The Terms of Political Discourse*. 2nd ed. Princeton: Princeton University Press, 1983.

Corbie-Smith G., S. B. Thomas, and D. M. St. George. "Distrust, Race, and Research." *Archives of Internal Medicine* 162, no. 21 (2002): 2458–63.

Covey, Russell. "Reconsidering the Relationship between Cognitive Psychology and Plea Bargaining." *Marquette Law Review* 91, no. 1 (2007): 213–47.

Crespigny, Anthony de. "Power and Its Forms." *Political Studies* 26, no. 2 (1968): 192–205.

Cryder, Cynthia E., Alex J. London, Kevin G. Volpp, and George Lowenstein. "Informative Inducement: Study Payment as a Signal of Risk." *Social Science and Medicine* 70, no. 3 (2010): 455–64.

Deci, Edward L., and Richard M. Ryan. *Intrinsic Motivation and Self-Determination in Human Behavior*. New York: Plenum Press, 1985.

Deci, Edward L., John Nezlek, and Louise Sheinman. "Characteristics of the Rewarder and Intrinsic Motivation of the Rewardee." *Journal of Personality and Social Psychology* 40, no. 1 (1981): 3–10.

Deci, Edward L., Richard Koestner, Richard M. Ryan, and Judy Cameron. "Extrinsic Rewards and Intrinsic Motivation in Education: Reconsidered Once Again: Comment/Reply." *Review of Educational Research* 71, no. 1 (2001): 1–27.

Dempsey, John R. "Taste of College Keeps Students in High School." *New York Times*, February 8, 2010, p. A14.

Devinat, Paul. "The American Labour Movement and Scientific Management." *International Labour Review* 13, no. 4 (1926): 461–88.

Dewey, John. *The Public and Its Problems*. Chicago: Swallow Press, 1954.

Dickert, Neal, and Christine Grady. "Incentives for Research Participants." In *Oxford Textbook of Clinical Research Ethics*, ed. Ezekiel J. Emanuel et al. New York: Oxford University Press, 2008.

———. "What's the Price of a Research Subject: Approaches to Payment for Research Participation." *New England Journal of Medicine* 341, no. 3 (1999): 198–203.

Dollar, David, and Aart Kraay. "Spreading the Wealth." *Foreign Affairs* 81, no. 1 (2002): 120–33.

Dollar, David, and Jacob Svensson. "What Explains the Success or Failure of Structural Adjustment Programmes?" *Economic Journal* 110, no. 466 (2000): 894–917.

Donaldson, Thomas. "The Ethics of Conditionality in International Debt." *Millennium: Journal of International Studies* 20, no. 2 (1991): 155–68.

Easterbrook, Frank H. "Criminal Procedure as a Market System." *Journal of Legal Studies* 12, no. 2 (1983): 289–332.

———. "Plea Bargaining as Compromise." *Yale Law Journal* 101, no. 8: Symposium on Punishment (1992): 1969–78.

Easterly, William. *The Elusive Quest for Growth: Economists' Adventures and Misadventures in the Tropics*. Cambridge, MA: MIT Press, 2002.

———. *The White Man's Burden: Why the West's Efforts to Aid the Rest Have Done So Much Ill and So Little Good*. Oxford: Oxford University Press, 2006.

Edelen, C. G. "Production with Incentive Pay." Detroit: Local 51, Educational Department, UAW-CIO, 1943/44.

Egbert, Donald Drew, and Stow Persons, eds. *Socialism and American Life*. Vol. 2. Princeton: Princeton University Press, 1952.

Elster, Jon, ed. *Ulysses and the Sirens: Studies in Rationality and Irrationality*. Cambridge: Cambridge University Press, 1979.

———. *Rational Choice*. Oxford: Basil Blackwell, 1986.

Emanuel, Ezekiel J. "Ending Concerns about Undue Inducement." *American Society of Law and Medicine* 32, no. 1 (2004): 100–106.

Emanuel, Ezekiel J., Xolani E. Currie, and Alan Herman. "Undue Inducement in Clinical Research in Developing Countries: Is It a Worry?" *Lancet* 366, no. 9482 (2005): 336–40.

Enrich, Peter D. "Saving the States from Themselves: Commerce Clause Constraints on State Tax Incentives for Business." *Harvard Law Review* 110, no. 2 (1996): 377–468.

Etzioni, Amitai. "Social Control: Organizational Aspects." In *International Encyclopedia of the Social Sciences*. Vol. 14. New York: Macmillan, 1968.

Faden, Ruth R., Tom L. Beauchamp, and Nancy M. P. King. *A History and Theory of Informed Consent*. New York: Oxford University Press, 1986.

Fearon, James D. "Rationalist Explanations for War." *International Organization* 49, no. 3 (1995): 379–414.

Fehr, Ernst, and Armin Falk. "Psychological Foundations of Incentives." Working paper no. 95, Working Paper Series ISSN 1424-0459. Institute for Empirical Research in Economics, University of Zurich, November 2001.

Feinberg, Joel. *Harm to Self*. New York: Oxford University Press, 1986.

Feldstein, Martin. "Refocusing the IMF." *Foreign Affairs* 77, no. 2 (1998): 20–33.

Fisher, Roger, and William Ury. *Getting to Yes: Negotiating Agreement without Giving In*, ed. Bruce Patton. 2nd ed. Boston: Houghton-Mifflin, 1991.

Fiske, Alan, and Phil E. Tetlock. "Taboo Trade-Offs: Constitutive Prerequisites for Social Life." In *Political Psychology: Cultural and Cross-Cultural Perspectives*, ed. Stanley A. Renshon and John Duckitt. London: MacMillan, 1999.

Flink, Cheryl, Ann K. Boggiano, Deborah S. Main, Mary Barrett, and Phyllis A. Katz. "Children's Achievement-Related Behaviors: The Role of Extrinsic and Intrinsic Motivational Orientations." In *Achievement and Motivation: A Social-Development Perspective*, ed. Ann K. Boggiano and Thane S. Pittman. Cambridge: Cambridge University Press, 1993.

Foucault, Michel. *Discipline and Punish: The Birth of the Prison.* Trans. Alan Sheridan. 2nd ed. New York: Vintage Books, 1995.

Frank, Robert H., Thomas Gilovich, and Dennis T. Regan. "Does Studying Economics Inhibit Cooperation?" *Journal of Economic Perspectives* 7, no. 2 (1993): 159–72.

Frey, Bruno. "A Constitution for Knaves Crowds Out Civic Virtues." *Economic Journal* 107, no. 443 (1997): 1043–53.

———. *Not Just for the Money: An Economic Theory of Personal Motivation.* Cheltenham, UK: Edward Elgar, 1997.

———. "Institutions and Morale: The Crowding Out Effect." In *Economics, Values and Organizations*, ed. A. Ben-Ner and L. Putterman. Cambridge: Cambridge University Press, 1998.

Fryer, Roland, Jr. "Financial Incentives and Student Achievement: Evidence from Randomized Trials." Working paper, 15898, National Bureau of Economic Research, 2010. http://www.nber.org/papers/w15898.

Gates, Albert. "Incentive Pay: The Speed-up New Style." New York: Workers Party, 1944/45.

Goldstein, Joseph. "For Harold Laswell: Some Reflections on Human Dignity, Entrapment, Informed Consent and the Plea Bargain." *Yale Law Journal* 84, no. 4 (1975): 683–703.

Goodin, Robert E. "Permissive Paternalism: In Defence of the Nanny State." *The Responsive Community* 1 (Summer 1991): 42–51.

Gorr, Michael. "The Morality of Plea Bargaining." *Social Theory and Practice* 26, no. 1 (2000): 129–51.

Grant, Ruth W. *John Locke's Liberalism.* Chicago: University of Chicago Press, 1987.

———. *Hypocrisy and Integrity: Machiavelli, Rousseau and the Ethics of Politics.* Chicago: University of Chicago Press, 1997.

———. "The Ethics of Incentives: Historical Origins and Contemporary Understandings." *Economics and Philosophy* 18 (April 2002): 111–39.

———. "Passions and Interests Revisited: The Psychological Foundations of Economics and Politics." *Public Choice* 137, no. 3/4 (2008): 451–61.

Grant, Ruth W., and Jeremy Sugarman. "Ethics in Human Subjects Research: Do Incentives Matter?" *Journal of Medicine and Philosophy* 29, no. 6 (2004): 717–38.

Grant, Ruth W., and Nathan Tarcov, eds. *John Locke: Some Thoughts Concerning Education and Of the Conduct of the Understanding.* Indianapolis: Hackett, 1996.

Green, Donald P., and Ian Shapiro, eds. *Pathologies of Rational Choice Theory*. New Haven: Yale University Press, 1994.

Gruber, Lloyd. *Ruling the World: Power Politics and the Rise of the Supranational Institutions*. Princeton: Princeton University Press, 2000.

Guidorizzi, Douglas D. "Comment: Should We Really 'Ban' Plea Bargaining? The Core Concerns of Plea Bargaining Critics." *Emory Law Journal* 47 (Spring 1998): 753–81.

Haber, Samuel. *Efficiency and Uplift: Scientific Management in the Progressive Era, 1890–1920*. Chicago: University of Chicago Press, 1964.

Habermas, Jürgen. *Moral Consciousness and Communicative Action*. Trans. Christian Lenhardt and Shierry Weber. Cambridge, MA: MIT Press, 1990.

Hamilton, Alexander, James Madison, and John Jay. *The Federalist Papers*, ed. Clinton Rossiter. New York: Signet Classics, 1969.

Hardin, Russell. "Blackmailing for Mutual Good." *University of Pennsylvania Law Review* 141, no. 5 (1993): 1787–1816.

Hayek, Friedrich A. *Collectivist Economic Planning*. 5th ed. London: Routledge and Kegan Paul Ltd., 1956.

Healy, Kieran. *Last Best Gifts: Altruism and the Market for Human Blood and Organs*. Chicago: University of Chicago Press, 2006.

Henry, Gary T., and Ross Rubenstein. "Paying for Grades: Impact of Merit-Based Financial Aid on Educational Quality." *Journal of Policy Analysis and Management* 21, no. 1 (2002): 93–109.

Heumann, Milton. "A Note on Plea Bargaining and Case Pressure." *Law and Society Review* 9, no. 3 (1975): 515–28.

———. "Author's Reply." *Law and Society Review* 13, no. 2 (1979): 650–53.

Hilgard, Ernest R., and Donald G. Marquis. *Hilgard and Marquis' Conditioning and Learning*, rev. Gregory A. Kimble. 2nd ed. New York: Appleton-Century-Crofts, 1961.

Hobbes, Thomas. *Leviathan*, ed. C. B. MacPherson. Harmondsworth, England: Penguin Books, 1968.

Hobson, John Atkinson. *Incentives in the New Industrial Order*. London: Leonard Parsons, 1922.

Hollinger, David A. "Money and Academic Freedom a Half-Century after McCarthyism: Universities amid the Force Fields of Capital." In *Unfettered Expression*, ed. P. G. Hollingsworth. Ann Arbor: University of Michigan Press, 2000.

Hoxie, Robert Franklin. *Scientific Management and Labor*. 2nd ed. New York: D. Appleton and Co., 1921.

Hylland, Aanund. "The Purpose and Significance of Social Choice Theory: Some General Remarks and an Application to the 'Lady Chatterley Problem.'" In *Foundations of Social Choice Theory*, ed. Jon Elster and Aanund Hylland. Cambridge: Cambridge University Press, 1986.

International Monetary Fund. "Conditionality in Fund-Supported Programs—Policy Issues." February 16, 2001. http://www.imf .org/external/np/pdr/cond/2001/eng/policy/021601.pdf.

———. "Conditionality in Fund-Supported Programs—Overview." February 20, 2001. http://www.imf.org/external/np/pdr/ cond/2001/eng/overview/.

———. "IMF Adopts Guidelines Regarding Governance Issues." IMF News Brief No. 97/15. August 4, 1997. http://www.imf.org/ external/np/sec/nb/1997/nb9715.htm.

———. "Guidelines on Conditionality." September 25, 2002. http:// www.imf.org/external/np/pdr/cond/2002/eng/guid/092302.pdf.

———. "Factsheet—IMF Conditionality." September 27, 2010. http:// www.imf.org/external/np/exr/facts/conditio.htm.

———. "IMF Overhauls Lending Framework." Press Release No. 09/85. March 24, 2009. http://www.imf.org/external/np/sec/ pr/2009/pr0985.htm.

Jackson, C. Kirabo. "A Stitch in Time: The Effects of a Novel Incentive-Based High-School Intervention on College Outcomes." Working paper 15722. National Bureau of Economic Research, 2009. http://www.nber.org/papers/w15722.pdf.

Jacob, Brian A., and Stephen D. Levitt. "Catching Cheating Teachers: The Results of an Unusual Experiment in Implementing Theory." In *Brookings-Wharton Papers on Urban Affairs*, ed. William G. Gale and Janet Rothenberg Pack. Washington, DC: Brookings Institution Press, 2003.

———. "Rotten Apples: An Investigation of the Prevalence and Predictors of Teacher Cheating." *Quarterly Journal of Economics* 118, no. 3 (2003): 843–77.

Jonas, Hans. "Philosophical Reflections on Experimenting with Human Subjects." *Daedalus* 98, no. 2 (1969): 219–47.

Julian, Liam. "But Wrong on Paying Students." *Washington Post*, August 31, 2008. http://www.washingtonpost.com/wp-dyn/ content/article/2008/08/29/AR2008082902711.html.

Kahn, Jeffrey P., Anna M. Mastroianni, and Jeremy Sugarman, eds. *Beyond Consent: Seeking Justice in Research*. New York: Oxford University Press, 1998.

Kant, Immanuel. *Groundwork for the Metaphysics of Morals.* Trans. James Ellington. Indianapolis: Hackett, 1981.

Katz, Leo. *Ill-Gotten Gains: Evasion, Blackmail, Fraud, and Kindred Puzzles of the Law.* Chicago: University of Chicago Press, 1996.

Killick, Tony, Ramani Gunatilaka, and Anna Marr. *Aid and the Political Economy of Policy Change.* London: Routledge, 1998.

Kipnis, Kenneth. "Criminal Justice and the Negotiated Plea." *Ethics* 86, no. 2 (1976): 93–106.

———. "A Critic's Rejoinder." *Law and Society Review* 13, no. 2 (1979): 555–64.

Kohn, Alfie. *Punished by Rewards: The Trouble with Gold Stars, Incentive Plans, A's, Praise and Other Bribes.* New York: Houghton Mifflin, 1993.

Kupperman, Joel. *Character.* New York: Oxford University Press, 1991.

Laidler, H. W. "Incentives under Capitalism and Socialism." New York: League for Industrial Democracy, 1933.

Langbein, John H. "Land without Plea Bargaining: How the Germans Do It." *Michigan Law Review* 78, no. 2 (1979): 204–25.

———. "Torture and Plea Bargaining." *The Public Interest* 58 (Winter 1980): 43–61.

Lazear, Edward P. "Incentive Contracts." In *The New Palgrave: A Dictionary of Economics,* ed. John Eatwell, Murray Milgate, and Peter Newman. New York: Stockton Press, 1987.

Lepore, Jill. "Not So Fast." *The New Yorker,* October 12, 2009, pp. 114–22.

Lepper, Mark R., David Greene, and Richard E. Nisbett. "Undermining Children's Intrinsic Interest with Extrinsic Rewards." *Journal of Personality Psychology* 28, no. 1 (1973): 129–37.

Levitt, Steven D., and Stephen J. Dubner. *Freakonomics: A Rogue Economist Explores the Hidden Side of Everything.* New York: Harper Collins, 2005.

Lippmann, Walter. *The Phantom Public.* New Brunswick, NJ: Transaction Publishers, 1993.

Locke, John. *Two Treatises of Government: A Critical Edition,* ed. Peter Laslett. Cambridge: Cambridge University Press, 1963.

London, Alex J. "Undue Inducements and Reasonable Risks: Will the Dismal Science Lead to Dismal Research Ethics?" *American Journal of Bioethics* 5, no. 5 (2005): 29–32.

Lyerly, Anne Drapkin, Margaret Olivia Little, and Ruth Faden. "The Second Wave: Toward Responsible Inclusion of Pregnant Women in Research." *International Journal of Feminist Approaches to Bioethics* 1, no. 2 (2008): 6–22.

Lyerly, Anne Drapkin, Lisa M. Mitchell, Elizabeth M. Armstrong, Lisa H. Harris, Rebecca Kukla, Miriam Kupperman, and Margaret Olivia Little. "Risks, Values, and Decision Making Surrounding Pregnancy." *Obstetrics and Gynecology* 109, no. 4 (2007): 979–84.

Lynch, David. "The Impropriety of Plea Agreements: A Tale of Two Counties." *Law and Social Inquiry* 19, no. 1 (1994): 115–33.

Machiavelli, Niccolo. *The Prince: A New Translation, Backgrounds, Interpretations, Peripherica*. New York: Norton, 1977.

MacIntyre, Alasdair. *After Virtue*. Notre Dame, IN: Notre Dame University Press, 1981.

Macklin, Ruth. "'Due' and 'Undue' Inducements: On Paying Money to Research Subjects." *IRB* 3, no. 5 (1981): 1–6.

———. "Response: Beyond Paternalism." *IRB* 4, no. 3 (1982): 6–7.

Mansfield, Carol, George Van Houtven, and Joel Huber. "Compensating for Public Harms: Why Public Goods Are Preferred to Money." *Land Economics* 78, no. 3 (2000): 368–89.

Margalit, Avishai. *Compromises and Rotten Compromises*. Princeton: Princeton University Press, 2009.

Mayo, Elton. *The Social Problems of an Industrial Civilization*. Boston: Harvard University Graduate School of Business, 1945.

———. *The Human Problems of an Industrial Civilization*. New York: Viking, 1960.

McGraw, Kenneth O. "The Detrimental Effects of Reward on Performance: A Literature Review and a Prediction Model." In *The Hidden Costs of Reward: New Perspectives on the Psychology of Human Motivation*, ed. Mark Lepper and David Greene. Hillsdale, NJ: Lawrence Erlbaum, 1978.

McNeill, Paul. "A Response to Wilkinson and Moore: Paying People to Participate in Research: Why Not?" *Bioethics* 11, no. 5 (1997): 390–96.

Mellström, Carl, and Magnus Johannesson. "Crowding Out in Blood Donation: Was Titmuss Right?" *Journal of the European Economic Association* 6, no. 4 (2008): 845–63.

Merriam, Charles. *Systematic Politics*. Chicago: University of Chicago Press, 1945.

———. *New Aspects of Politics*. 3rd ed. Chicago: University of Chicago Press, 1970.

Midgley, Carol, Avi Kaplan, and Michael Middleton. "Performance-Approach Goals: Good for What, for Whom, under What Circumstances, and at What Cost?" *Journal of Educational Psychology* 93, no. 1 (2001): 77–86.

Miller, Dale T. "The Norm of Self-Interest." *American Psychologist* 54, no. 12 (1999): 1053–60.

Miller, Robert H., and Harold S. Luft. "Does Managed Care Lead to Better or Worse Quality of Care?" *Health Affairs* 16, no. 5 (1997): 7–25.

Mills, John A. *Control: A History of Behavioral Psychology*. New York: New York University Press, 1998.

Milner, Helen V. "Review: Globalization, Development, and International Institutions: Normative and Positive Perspectives." *Perspectives on Politics* 3, no. 4 (2005): 833–54.

Moe, Terry M. "Power and Political Institutions." *Perspectives on Politics* 3, no. 2 (2005): 215–33.

Moreno, J. D. "Convenient and Captive Populations." In *Beyond Consent: Seeking Justice in Research*, ed. J. P. Kahn, A. M. Mastroianni, and J. Sugarman. New York: Oxford University Press, 1998.

Mumford, Lewis. *Technics and Civilization*. New York: Harcourt, Brace and Co., 1934.

Nelkin, D., and L. Andrews. "Homo Economicus: Commercialization of Body Tissue in the Age of Biotechnology." *Hastings Center Report* 28 (1998): 30–39.

Nelson, Daniel. *Frederick W. Taylor and the Rise of Scientific Management*. Madison: University of Wisconsin Press, 1980.

Nelson, R. M. "Children as Research Subjects." In *Beyond Consent: Seeking Justice in Research*, ed. J. P. Kahn, A. M. Mastroianni, and J. Sugarman. New York: Oxford University Press, 1998.

Newton, Lisa. "Inducement, Due and Otherwise." *IRB* 4, no. 3 (1982): 4–6.

Niou, Emerson N. S., and Peter C. Ordeshook. "Universalism in Congress," *American Journal of Political Science* 29, no. 2 (1985): 246–58.

Norris, Floyd. "Fraying at the Edges." *New York Times*, February 4, 2010, B8.

Nozick, Robert. "Coercion." In *Philosophy, Politics and Society*, ed. Peter Laslett, W. G. Runciman, and Quentin Skinner. Oxford: Blackwell, 1972.

Nussbaum, Martha. *Frontiers of Justice: Disability, Nationality, Species Membership*. Cambridge, MA: Harvard University Press, 2006.

Nye, Joseph. *Soft Power: The Means to Success in World Politics*. New York: Public Affairs Press, 2004.

O'Connor, Ellen S. "The Politics of Management Thought: A Case Study of the Harvard Business School and the Human Relations School." *Academy of Management Review* 24, no. 1 (1999): 117–31.

O'Donnell, John. *The Origins of Behaviorism: American Psychology, 1870–1920.* New York: New York University Press, 1985.

Olson, Mancur. *The Logic of Collective Action: Public Goods and the Theory of Groups.* Cambridge, MA: Harvard University Press, 1971.

Pastore, Ann L., and Kathleen Maguire, eds. *Sourcebook of Criminal Justice Statistics: 1999.* Washington, DC: U.S. Department of Justice, Bureau of Justice Statistics, 1999.

Pearson, Steven D., James E. Sabin, and Ezekiel J. Emmanuel. "Ethical Guidelines for Physician Compensation Based on Capitation." *New England Journal of Medicine* 339, no. 10 (1998): 689–93.

Pettifor, Ann. "Resolving International Debt Crises Fairly." *Ethics and International Affairs* 17, no. 2 (2003): 2–9.

Philips, Michael. "The Question of Voluntariness in the Plea Bargaining Controversy: A Philosophical Clarification." *Law and Society Review* 16, no. 2 (1981): 207–24.

Pink, Daniel H. *Drive: The Surprising Truth about What Motivates Us.* New York: Riverhead Books, 2009.

Pitts, Jesse R. "Social Control: The Concept." In *International Encyclopedia of the Social Sciences*, vol. 16, ed. D. L. Stills. New York: Macmillan, 1968.

Pogge, Thomas. "The Moral Demands of Global Justice." *Dissent* 47, no. 4 (2000): 37–42.

———. *World Poverty and Human Rights.* Malden, MA: Polity Press, 2008.

Posner, Richard A. "The Immoralist (Review of *Ill-Gotten Gains: Evasion, Blackmail, Fraud, and Kindred Puzzles of the Law*)." *New Republic*, July 15–22, 1996, pp. 38–41.

Ramsey, Richard David. "Morning Star: The Values-Communication of Skinner's *Walden Two*." Ph.D. thesis, Rensselaer Polytechnic Institute, 1979.

Rawls, John. *The Law of Peoples.* Cambridge, MA: Harvard University Press, 1999.

Raymond, Margaret. "Paying for A's: An Early Exploration of Student Reward and Incentive Programs in Charter Schools." Paper presented to the CESifo/PEPG Conference "Economic Incentives: Do They Work in Education? Insights and Findings from Behavioral Research." Munich, Germany, May 16–17, 2008.

Reddy, Sanjay G. "International Debt: The Constructive Implications of Some Moral Mathematics." *Ethics and International Affairs* 21, no. 1 (2007): 81–92.

Reeve, Andrew. *Modern Theories of Exploitation*. London: Sage, 1987.

Reich, Rob. "A Failure of Philanthropy: American Charity Short-changes the Poor, and Public Policy Is Partly to Blame." *Stanford Social Innovation Review* 3, no. 4 (2005): 24–33.

———. "Toward a Political Theory of Philanthropy." In *Giving Well: The Ethics of Philanthropy*, ed. Patricia Illingworth, Thomas Pogge, and Leif Wenar. Oxford: Oxford University Press, 2010.

Remmer, Karen L. "The Politics of Economic Stabilization: IMF Standby Programs in Latin America, 1954–1984." *Comparative Politics* 19, no. 1 (1986): 1–24.

Riker, William H. *The Art of Political Manipulation*. New Haven: Yale University Press, 1986.

Ripley, Amanda. "Should Kids Be Bribed to Do Well in School?" *Time*, April 19, 2010, pp. 40–47.

Roback, A. A. *Behaviorism at Twenty-Five*. Boston: Sci-Art Publishers, 1937.

Roemer, John. "Should Marxists Be Interested in Exploitation?" In *Analytical Matters*, ed. John Roemer. Cambridge: Cambridge University Press, 1986.

Rosen, Jeffrey. "Prisoners of Parole." *New York Times Magazine*, January 10, 2010, pp. 37–39.

Ross, Dorothy. *The Origins of American Social Science*. Cambridge: Cambridge University Press, 1991.

Ross, Edward A. *Social Control: A Survey of the Foundations of Order*. New York: Macmillan, 1901.

Ryan, Richard M., and Edward L. Deci. "When Paradigms Clash: Comments on Cameron and Pierce's Claim That Rewards Do Not Undermine Intrinsic Motivation." *Review of Educational Research* 66, no. 1 (1996): 33–38.

Sachs, Jeffrey. "Conditionality, Debt Relief, and the Developing Country Debt Crisis." Working paper 2644. National Bureau of Economic Research, 1988. http://www.nber.org/papers/w2644.

Sansone, Carol, and Judith M. Harackiewicz, eds. *Intrinsic and Extrinsic Motivation: The Search for Optimal Motivation and Performance*. San Diego: Academic Press, 2000.

Schachter, Hindy Lauer. *Frederick Taylor and the Public Administration Community: A Reevaluation*. Albany: SUNY Press, 1989.

Schaefer, G. Owen, Ezekiel J. Emanuel, and Alan Wertheimer. "The

Obligation to Participate in Biomedical Research." *Journal of the American Medical Association* 302, no. 1 (2009): 67–72.

Schelling, Thomas C. *Arms and Influence*. New Haven: Yale University Press, 1966.

Schulhofer, Stephen J. "Is Plea Bargaining Inevitable?" *Harvard Law Review* 97, no. 5 (1984): 1037–1107.

———. "Plea Bargaining as Disaster." *Yale Law Journal* 101, no. 8: Symposium on Punishment (1992): 1979–2009.

———. "A Wake-Up Call from the Plea Bargaining Trenches." *Law and Social Inquiry* 19, no. 1 (1994): 135–44.

Schwartz, Barry. *The Battle for Human Nature: Science, Morality and Modern Life*. New York: W. W. Norton, 1986.

———. *The Costs of Living: How Market Freedom Erodes the Best Things in Life*. New York: W. W. Norton, 1994.

Schwartz, Barry, Richard Schuldenfrei, and Hugh Lacey. "Operant Psychology as Factory Psychology." *Behaviorism* 6, no. 2 (1978): 229–54.

Scott, Robert E., and William J. Stuntz. "Plea Bargaining as Contract." *Yale Law Journal* 101, no. 8: Symposium on Punishment (1992): 1909–68.

Scott-Clayton, Judith. "On Money and Motivation: A Quasi-Experimental Analysis of Financial Incentives for College Achievement." Unpublished paper. Columbia University Teachers College, 2009.

Seidelman, Raymond. *Disenchanted Realists: Political Science and the American Crisis, 1884–1984*. Albany: SUNY Press, 1985.

Sen, Amartya. *Development as Freedom*. New York: Anchor Books, 1999.

Singer, Peter. "Altruism and Commerce: A Defense of Titmuss against Arrow." *Philosophy and Public Affairs* 2, no. 3 (1973): 312–20.

Skinner, B. F. *Walden Two*. New York: Macmillan, 1948.

———. *About Behaviorism*. New York: A. F. Knopf, 1974.

Slavin, Robert E. "Can Financial Incentives Enhance Educational Outcomes? Evidence from International Experiments." Unpublished paper. Institute for Effective Education, University of York, 2009.

Smelser, Neil J. "The Rational Choice Perspective: A Theoretical Assessment." *Rationality and Society* 4 , no. 4 (1992): 381–410.

Smith, Adam. *The Wealth of Nations*, ed. Edwin Cannan. Chicago: University of Chicago Press, 1976.

———. *The Theory of Moral Sentiments*. Indianapolis: Liberty Fund Press, 2009.

Smith, Laurence, and William Woodward, eds. *B. F. Skinner and Behaviorism in American Culture*. Bethlehem, PA: Lehigh University Press, 1996.

Snoy, Bernard. "Ethical Issues in International Lending." *Journal of Business Ethics* 8, no. 8 (1989): 635–39.

Sophocles. *Philoctetes*. In *Sophocles II: Ajax, The Women of Trachis, Electra & Philoctetes*, ed. David Grene and Richard Lattimore. Chicago: University of Chicago Press, 1969.

Sorenson, George. "Conditionality, Democracy and Development." In *Aid and Political Conditionality*, ed. Olav Stokke. London: Frank Cass, 1995.

Spencer, Margaret B., Elizabeth Noll, and Elaine Cassidy. "Monetary Incentives in Support of Academic Achievement: Results of a Randomized Field Trial Involving High-Achieving, Low-Resource, Ethnically Diverse Urban Adolescents." *Evaluation Review* 29, no. 3 (2005): 199–222.

Spragens, Thomas A., Jr. "Is the Enlightenment Project Worth Saving?" *Modern Age* 43, no. 1 (2001): 49–60.

———. *Getting the Left Right: The Transformation, Decline, and Reformation of American Liberalism*. Lawrence: University Press of Kansas, 2009.

Staddon, John. *The New Behaviorism: Mind, Mechanism, and Society*. Philadelphia: Psychology Press, 2000.

Steiner, Hillel. "Individual Liberty." *Proceedings of the Aristotelian Society*, n.s., 75 (1974–75): 33–50.

Stigler, George J., and Gary Becker. "De Gustibus Non Disputandum." *American Economic Review* 67, no. 2 (1977): 76–90.

Stiglitz, Joseph E. *Globalization and Its Discontents*. New York: W. W. Norton, 2002.

———. "Ethics, Market and Government Failure, and Globalization." In *Sovereign Debt at the Crossroads*, ed. Chris Jochnick and Fraser A. Preston. Oxford: Oxford University Press, 2006.

Stokke, Olav, ed. *Aid and Political Conditionality*. London: Frank Cass, 1995.

Surjadinata, Kenneth. "Comment: Revisiting Corrupt Practices from a Market Perspective." *Emory International Law Review* 12 (Spring 1998): 1021–90.

Taylor, Frederick W. "Shop Management." In *The Principles of Scientific Management and Shop Management*. London: Routlege/Thoemmes Press, 1993.

Taylor, Robert. "A Kantian Defense of Self-Ownership." *Journal of Political Philosophy* 12, no. 1 (2004): 65–78.

Thacker, Strom C. "The High Politics of IMF Lending." *World Politics* 52, no. 1 (1999): 38–75.

Thaler, Richard H., and Cass R. Sunstein. *Nudge: Improving Decisions about Health, Wealth, and Happiness.* New Haven: Yale University Press, 2008.

Thucydides. *History of the Peloponnesian War.* Trans. Rex Warner. Harmondsworth, England: Penguin Books, 1972.

Tishler, C. L., and S. Bartholomae. "The Recruitment of Normal Healthy Volunteers: A Review of the Literature on the Use of Financial Incentives." *Journal of Clinical Pharmacology* 42, no. 4 (2002): 365–73.

Titmuss, Richard. *The Gift Relationship.* New York: The New Press, 1997.

Trebilcock, Michael J. *The Limits of Freedom of Contract.* Cambridge, MA: Harvard University Press, 1993.

U.S. Department of Health, Education, and Welfare. National Commission for the Protection of Human Subjects of Biomedical and Behavioral Research. *The Belmont Report: Ethical Principles and Guidelines for the Protection of Human Subjects of Research.* Washington, DC: U.S. GPO, 1979.

Urdan, Tim. "Intrinsic Motivation, Extrinsic Rewards, and Divergent Views of Reality." *Educational Psychology Review* 15, no. 3 (2003): 311–25.

Urwick, Lyndall F. *The Life and Work of Elton Mayo.* London: Urwick, Orr and Partners, Ltd., 1960.

Van de Veer, Donald. *Paternalistic Intervention: The Moral Bounds on Benevolence.* Princeton: Princeton University Press, 1986.

Vreeland, James. *The International Monetary Fund: Politics of Conditional Lending.* London: Routledge, 2007.

———. "The IMF and Economic Development." In *Reinventing Foreign Aid*, ed. William Easterly. Cambridge, MA: MIT Press, 2008.

Wagner, R. Harrison. *War and the State: The Theory of International Politics.* Ann Arbor: University of Michigan Press, 2007.

Walzer, Michael. *Spheres of Justice: A Defense of Pluralism and Equality.* New York: Basic Books, 1983.

Watson, John B. "Psychology as the Behaviorist Views It." *Psychological Review* 20, no. 2 (1913): 158–77.

———. *Behaviorism.* New York: W. W. Norton, 1924.

Watson, John B., and William MacDougal. *The Battle of Behaviorism: An Exposition and an Exposure.* New York: W. W. Norton, 1929.

Weingast, Barry. "A Rational Choice Perspective on Congressional Norms." *American Journal of Political Science* 23, no. 2 (1979): 245–62.

Wertheimer, Alan. "Freedom, Morality, Plea Bargaining and the Supreme Court." *Philosophy and Public Affairs* 8, no. 3 (1979): 203–34.

———. "The Prosecutor and the Gunman." *Ethics* 89, no. 3 (1979): 269–79.

———. *Coercion.* Princeton: Princeton University Press, 1987.

———. *Exploitation.* Princeton: Princeton University Press, 1996.

Wertheimer, Alan, and Franklin G. Miller. "Payment for Research Participation: A Coercive Offer?" *Journal of Medical Ethics* 34, no. 5 (2008): 389–92.

Westbrook, Robert B. *John Dewey and American Democracy.* Ithaca: Cornell University Press, 1993.

Wilkinson, M., and A. Moore. "Inducement in Research." *Bioethics* 11, no. 5 (1997): 373–89.

Willett, Thomas D. "Understanding the IMF Debate." *The Independent Review* 5, no. 4 (2001): 593–610.

Winthrop, John. "A Model of Christian Charity." In *Winthrop Papers*, 6 vols., ed. Allyn Bailey Forbes et al. Boston: Massachusetts Historical Society, 1929.

Wood, Allen W. *Kantian Ethics.* Cambridge: Cambridge University Press, 2008.

World Medical Association. *Declaration of Helsinki.* http://www.wma.net/en/30publications/10policies/b3/index.html.

Zacharias, Fred C. "Justice in Plea Bargaining." *William and Mary Law Review* 1122, no. 39 (1998): 1127–35.

Zimmerman, David. "More on Coercive Wage Offers: A Reply to Alexander." *Philosophy and Public Affairs* 10, no. 2 (1981): 121–45.

Index